Thought Leadership with Theory of Zero Salary

(With Training Modules)

Enterprise Level Calibration of Thoughts and Meditation

First Edition

Author:

Ankur Chaturvedi

(with Inspiration from BK Jagdish Chandra Hasija)

Copyright©2018 by Author, All Rights Reserved

About the Author

Author is a founder of Secretum Presidente Clothing LLP and provided its Quality Consulting services to Infosys, HSBC, Patni Computers, American Express. He is a post graduate and certified individual from ASQ (American Society of Quality), Cisco and IIT Delhi, with a professional experience of 12 years.

And practicing meditation for the last 20 years.

Dedication

I would like to dedicate this book to B.k. Jagdish Chandra Hasija, who is one of founding member of Prajapita Brahma Kumaris. His lectures, books have been a great inspiration towards my life and for this Book. I am astonished by the amount of inter-disciplinary knowledge that he had in regard to the concept of meditation, which has completely changed the paradigm of my life for good. This book is my expression of gratitude towards him and society for betterment. I cannot thank enough in words.

Secondly, I would like to thank to my family as they never stopped believing in me. Lastly but not the least, to my beautiful wife, who has always inspired me to achieve great things. Only because of you, I could able to write my first book ☺

Table of Contents

---------------------------Part 1-------------------------------

Chapter 1. Introduction: Theory of Zero Salary vis a vis Happiness at Work

Chapter 2. Fundamentals of Theory of Zero Salary

---------------------------Part 2-------------------------------

Chapter 3. Surgical analysis to Thoughts and Meditation

    3.1 Training module 1: Physics Behind Meditation

    3.2 Training module 2: Application of Meditation

Chapter 4. Defining and Measuring the Extent of Hazards of Poor Culture

---------------------------Part 3-------------------------------

Chapter 5. Planting a solution:

    5.1 Cultural Fit

    5.2 Milagro: Power of consciousness:

    5.3 Renovatio

    5.4 Sentido: Building crystal clear thinking

    5.5 Serenidad: Non-Judgmental Attitude

    5.6 Mindfulness: Deploying Meditation at an Organizational level:

    5.7 Institutionalize the respect for company:

    5.8 Transforming into positive Personality

    5.9 Developing Innovation and Creative Capabilities

5.10 Trust between employees and Employer (Job Security)

5.11 Controlling Attrition (Case Study)

5.12 Delivering Job Satisfaction by controlling thoughts

5.13 How to be OK when it is not OK (Emotional Intelligence)

5.14 Psychological twins

5.15 Eradicate Negative politics from work culture

5.16 Servant leadership (Employees are new Customers)

5.17 Cariño: Positive self-talk

5.18 Bell Curve, a Malpractice or best practice

5.19 Increasing IQ of the Employees

5.20 Majo: Focus on Grooming, Productivity and Accuracy will follow

5.21 Improving appraisal system

5.22 Déjà vu of Errors

5.23 Relaxing at office, a malpractice or ice breaker

------------------------------Part 4-----------------------------

Chapter 6. Control: Not letting the hard work go

6.1 Drainage of thoughts and Risk Team

6.1.1 Expending Risk Team's profile

6.2 Extending BCP (Business continuity planning) Team's profile

Appendix

How to Read This Book

In this book, I have designed my approach to derive observations coming from logical thinking and not to touch the chord of debate. Because I want to keep it for the last and did not want to lose the focus. All your concerns should get resolved by the time, you finish reading this book.

In the field of Business Quality consulting, the most difficult subject is, driving culture (i.e. Lean concept on people or resolving will issue of the people) because it involves so many factors and easy to get lost in the subject. In the era of process improvements, we always talk about standardization of work. Likewise, in this book, we will be talking about standardization of thoughts.

I have been a great admirer of Hollywood movies and deeply inspired from Meditation. In good Hollywood movies, generally you don't get to see the complete plot, in fact first half looks ordinary & unstructured and then in the second half they show you the extraordinary. As you progress reading in the book, I will continue to challenge status quo and proposing new standards which will raise the bar to next level. Does not matter, how impossible it looks to you, I will start with relevant research accompanied with transformation process. I have kept wow factors in each topic and taken examples/theories mostly from corporate, sports, spirtualty, philosophy,

Medical science, psychology and history to make it relevant.

My job here is think the unthinkable. I have tried to give you the ideal situations so that you have a vision while dealing with these kind of situations. Theory of Zero salary is such a vast topic, I have tried cover touching every aspect with focused approach.

Mostly, management theories and matrix are based on identifying behavioral traits of the employees and then calibrating it. Whereas this approach is about getting into the root of the problem and transforming the people's behavior by implementing the solutions with clinical approach. It also describes the complete process of transformation.

Lastly, use of the words his, her does not describe my biasedness towards any gender. Please consider these words as genderless.

Preface

What next: Theory of Zero Salary

Market is flooded with the books on enhancing mind powers of individuals. This book focuses on deploying mind power techniques across organization and using them for business benefits.

Often organizations call consultants or in-house Quality teams for process improvements, the most common phenomenon is they do the improvement but could not sustain. The primary reason for non-sustenance is consultants never been able to remove the seeds of the problems, which is the culture. Looking only the process data and not working on culture, is like cutting branches of a tree instead of seed. That is where this book is different, not only it highlights the business perspective of culture it also talks about the process of transformation.

Additionally, with every minute, the world is increasing its degree of competitiveness, Clients are demanding not just contractual commitments but also productivity benefits, employees are expecting not just a work place but a place to be in, employee's loyalty is going down, you just invented something today and tomorrow it became a culture, technology changes are sky rocketing the consumer expectations, macro factors are turbulent and disruptive etc. NOKIA, HMT, BAJAJ, MURPHY, RAJDOOT and AMBASDOR are some names to take which were unable to survive because they did not embrace change or could not leverage their resources.

To conquer some of the above listed problems, we already have Lean, Six Sigma, Capacity Modelling, Hoshin Kanri etc. these theories deals in extrinsic approach and resolution whereas Theory of zero Salary follows an intrinsic approach and lot finer and gives us an altogether different perspective for organizational culture. In this approach, we believe that most important resource for an organization is its employee's **"Thoughts"** which subsequently leads to Values & Action. Measuring Organizational culture is nothing but quantifying the thoughts. Thoughts are responsible for all the actions.

This approach talks about **D**efine, **M**easuring, **P**lanting and **C**ontrolling thoughts derived from organization's mission and vision.

About its practical application, only one organization who has successfully leveraged this feature. And it is the biggest wonder to me because no matter how much money you have you just can't replicate its business model.

Adding cherry to cake, the organization does not provide any additional monetary services to its employees means it is free of cost. This does mean that an organization does not have to reinvent the wheel or invest heavily to gain this business edge.

This book is all about giving you a vision of leveraging current resources to meet future demands. It is not a work of philosophy or theory *rather it is a case wherein i have tried to use true facts, logical thinking from various disciplines (i.e. Science, Management, Philosophy etc) to bridge the gap between how business runs vs what science and spirituality implies.*

The approach of the book is as follows, phase 1 is referring to basic or elementary definition of the subject, its parameters, business/process/quality metrics it involves, impacts.

Phase 2 is an advanced stage to phase 1, it will try and cover the future state of the process or people or industry. In this phase, I introduce some new concepts derived from most common logical thinking. We have used pragmatic and practical approach to implement and control various tools and methodologies. In case you think, you have any different opinion, you are welcome to approach Author.

---------------------Part 1-----------------------

INTRODUCTION

Chapter 1. Introduction: Theory of Zero Salary vis a vis Happiness at Work

Chapter 2. Fundamentals of Theory of Zero Salary

Chapter 1

Introduction: Theory of Zero Salary vis a vis Happiness at Work

In business, we measure and control every business asset with some or other metric. For example, we control our financials accuracy, measure productivity and accuracy of employees, keep a check on inventory etc. one thing which we forgot to control is the most basic thing, i.e. "Thought". Which is the most basic fundamental unit of the universe. Theory of zero salary prescribe methods to measure, plant and control the thoughts of the employees.

The importance of thoughts is of far more concern than Net profit figure to any organization, because it has the power to make or break your organization. If the thoughts of business owner and its employees are not calibrated, then the business can only leverage only 5 or 10% of its overall potential. Compounding effect of all the employees' thoughts is termed as organizational culture. Irony with culture is, you have to make consistent focused efforts for a thriving culture. It is the backbone of any organization, and is the reason, why same employee was working at par with its previous company and now doing wonders with the new one. Power to influence the thoughts can result into great benefits which we can ever think of, for example, we can manifest loyalty, satisfaction, creativity, innovation, happiness, productivity etc.

Let's start with happiness first, [1] Employee happiness has increasingly become an imperative in business. Why? There is now growing evidence that when one's employees are happy, organizations thrive. One study found that happy employees are up to 20% more productive than unhappy employees. When it comes to salespeople, happiness has an even greater impact, raising sales by 37%. But the benefits don't end there.

Happy employees are also good news for organizations: The stock prices of Fortune's "100 Best Companies to Work for" rose 14% per year from 1998 to 2005, while companies not on the list only reported a 6% increase. While job security and financial stability are important to job satisfaction, so are opportunities to use one's skills and abilities. The bottom line is that people need to continue to grow in order to remain engaged and productive. Happiness is linked to productivity. But what does it mean to be "happy" in the workplace? That is where the role of Theory of Zero Salary comes into the picture.

As we have understood the importance of employee happiness, the question is, how to measure and increase it. What are the other common factors that complement employee happiness and how can these factors be monetized?

That is where the Theory of Zero Salary comes into the picture. Theory talks about the initiatives to manifest happiness and loyalty among employees along with its impact on business metrics and leveraging their intellectual faculties for the business. It outlines the significance of employee happiness, satisfaction, variation of thoughts across organization and techniques to enrich these metrics. It follows a pragmatic approach to bring an organization in black hole grid (discussed in next chapter).

As suggested by HR directors of some of Britain's top companies, "it's not as simple as it sounds, because great culture is usually a combination of a vast number of elements." Theory helps us in simplifying the riddle of how to improve organization culture. General assumption is, organization needs to invest colossal time and money which is not feasible in current market conditions as everybody is looking for cost benefits. Let's start looking at below examples:

Case 1: Infosys, Microsoft and Google have created their own campuses (which is an investment). These companies invest heavily in employee benefits. American Express also gives hefty monetary benefits to earn loyalty, tenure and employee satisfaction.

Case 2: On the contrary, there are some organizations who pay very less or moderate and still achieve above benefits, for example, Mumbai Dabba Wala, Defense Forces etc.

Case 3: These organizations does not give money at all. People just come, work and go back home. Employee's health and satisfaction is at the peak. These are nothing but spiritual organizations.

This is an interesting observation as we are moving from Case 1 to 3, salary is decreasing (in fact, it has gone to zero) and satisfaction & Health is crowning. This mark the origination of Theory of Zero Salary. The theory is pragmatic approach of measuring and leveraging the most valuable asset of the organization (i.e. Employee's thought) by institutionalizing the concept of Meditation.

Theory follows a tops to bottom approach, prescribe measures and idealize an organization environment where employee love to come to office than home to the extent he is ready to work for free if situations calls for it. Thus helping business creating a niche advantage. The approach talks about Define, Measuring, Planting and Controlling thoughts derived from organization's mission and vision. Includes practice to improve cognizant abilities of employees.

Chapter 2

Fundamentals of Theory of Zero Salary

The objective is to make organization's culture so conducive that employee should be ready to work for free and his/her thoughts, behavior and actions should remain aligned with organizational objective.

Law: *variation in thoughts is a financial crime for an organization. To develop exotic business edge, all employee's thoughts needs to be focused.*

Imagine all productions and operations department heads along with business owner are sitting on a common shell boat and with every inch forward, the company is earning revenue or increasing market capitalization. Scientifically, for a boat to move forward, everybody has to row at right time, strength and motion. If these events are not aligned, either the boat will stay at same place or move backward.

This is also true in our corporate world, if business strategy has not penetrated at deepest level then people will not accept the change and eventually, it will fail. Cycle time for implementing a change will be elongated, by the time, it will get implemented, it will lose its business edge. By default, employees will remain frustrated with policies, management, work culture (almost every other thing), customers will have unrealistic demands because of trust deficit. Every day is somebody's doom's day. Everybody is an expert in blaming others and can write a book on "How to say no without saying No" etc. it does not matter, which consultant or employee you hire, the problem remains as is. Question is, how to resolve it?

Let's look at the fundamentals of the theory which is based on pyramid of transformation. Which has 3 divisions.

Section 3 called **Galaxy**. Like there are so many stars in galaxy roaming everywhere (with no alignment at all), this section pertains to employees who are not aligned with company priorities. Which depicts that variation of thoughts between the stakeholders is highest. Employees (i.e. Middle and Junior) hardly knows about the company's senior leadership priorities, vision, mission and policies. The information or awareness fail to infiltrate to lowest hierarchy. If an organization is dropping in this section, then the organization's ability to grow swiftly is substantially shrunk. How can we expect our employees to contribute towards organizational growth if they do not know the goals itself? In such organizations, the senior leadership will be completely oblivious of operation's problems. Employee will not feel connected with company policies and initiatives. There is a greater chance that leadership programs will not cater to ground reality at all, generating dissatisfaction among employees and management.

Section 2 called **solar system**, each planet has got its gravitational pull so they move in orbit, can't get closer to each other but remain equidistant (orbits are fixed). In this section stakeholders are aligned but have conflicting interest that keeps them apart and shows resistance in implementing company policies and changes. Employees knows the priorities of the management but they make sure that the changes are not implemented, they will always have a diplomatic answer as to why this change can't be implemented. The variation of thoughts is generally reduced as compared to previous section but could not converge to single thought.

Section 1 called **Black hole**, black hole is a place where the gravitational pull is so high that even light can't escape its surface. Its surface is densely squeezed to its core so eventually it is only the core that is left. Symbolizing to the highest concentration of material.

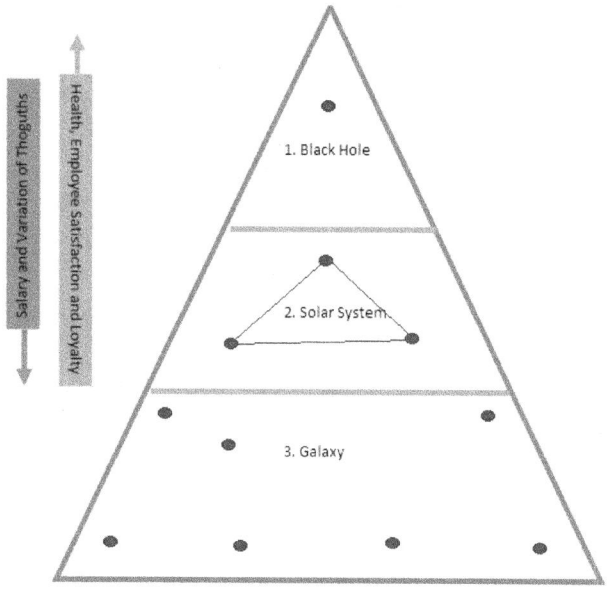

- Members in this section are dedicated to one single thought of organizational growth as they are emotionally attached to the organization not just for monetary gains.

- Resistance among employees is minimum as their values and thinking pattern are aligned,
- People prefer to stay in office than at home,
- Respect for the company is as good as nation,
- Innovation, creativity and hard work is rewarded
- Employees trust organization, they are willing to work even if it is not capable of paying their salaries on-time
- Job satisfaction is at its utmost peak

This is the ideal section to have for any organization. Coming back to the shell boat example, all employees across hierarchy are in synch. they clearly understand the goals of higher management. Hard/smart working guys are rewarded. People are happy. Senior leadership is concerned about the employee welfare. People like to work in such a company. Investors trust is tall.

Measures proposed in Theory of zero salary are intend to bring all employees of organization in black hole grid. You could notice that as you moving up in the pyramid, the salary and variation of thoughts among employees are decreasing whereas health, employee satisfaction and loyalty is increasing. It is the dream zone for every company to be in black hole, it gives them better efficiencies, phenomenal productivity of employees, happiness at work, pool of loyal employees, competitive edge of having skillful people and their longevity etc. In the following chapters, we will talk about the enterprise level initiatives to bring organization in the black hole lattice.

----------------------Part 2----------------------

TRAINING MATERIAL

Chapter 3. Surgical analysis to Thoughts and Meditation

      3.1 Training module: day 1

      3.2 Training module: day 2

Chapter 4. Defining and Measuring the Extent of Hazards of Poor Culture

----

Chapter 3

Surgical Analysis to Thoughts and Meditation

[2]Some of the examples of Meditation in business are, "Ray Dalio, founder of Bridgewater Associates, wrote in his book Principles: "I came to meditation in my own life during a very stressful work period that then turned into a very stressful personal period. But it freed me from so much pain. It completely inverted my entire point of view on life. I've been meditating consistently….and I've seen an exponential impact. In terms of scale, the more you do the greater the reward. More than linear."

Marc Benioff, co-founder and CEO of Salesforce.com, mentioned in an interview with the San Francisco Chronicle: "I am very interested in keeping a clear head. So I enjoy meditation, which I've been doing for over a decade - probably to help relieve the stress I was going through when I was working at Oracle."

Fred Wilson, a successful venture capitalist and co-founder of Union Square Ventures, wrote in his newsletter: "I've been meditating for ten to fifteen minutes every day for the past two months. I am experiencing a number of benefits but the one I am most cognizant of is an increased ability to avoid distraction in a conversation or some other situation where I need to be focused. I've always been good at being focused, sometimes to a fault. But I also find my mind wandering in situations where I am losing interest and that's obviously very bad. Meditation is like repetitive exercise of the focus muscle in the brain. So if you are having trouble being present in situations you want to be but can't, I would strongly recommend trying meditation. It's helped me with this and I imagine it will help you too.""

Finest inventions in the history of mankind has happened when we are able to explore the most basic element of creation. Atomic and Nuclear bombs are some of the examples. Similarly, thoughts are subtlest unit of universe which is responsible for what and where we are. The world around us is a result of our thoughts. Every thought generates a vibrating energy (i.e. negative or positive). Thoughts are incredible source of energy but if it is channelized properly, it can do a severe damage as well. Robbery, kidnapping, rapes, murders, phobias, depression are just few example of its ill effects. In the next few chapters, we are going to cover the training module for meditation.

Chapter 3.1

Training module 1: Physics behind Meditation

World is nothing but the result of our thoughts and actions. Let's stop for a moment and contemplate about it. What kind of a world, we are currently living in, what future that we are going to pass on to our generations?

Close to 800 000 people die due to suicide every year, which is one person every 40 seconds. Many more attempt suicide. Suicide occurs throughout the lifespan and is the second leading cause of death among 15-29 year olds globally. The question is, as we are moving towards technological arena, we are getting more and more stressed. The world is becoming a difficult battle. Meanwhile, human has crossed all lowest boundaries of humanity. People have lost their faith in humanity, relationships, values etc. we are losing the longevity and trust in our relationships. Sex lust is dominant that people have actually lost control over it. Almost every one of us has one or other fear. Lower middle class has a fear of losing jobs and business. Upper middle class is afraid of anti-social elements, income tax etc. Terrorism is another threat for all species. People are getting heart attacks at early ages. Kids are suffering from depression. Countries are ready to fight 3rd world war. Despite having all sorts of knowledge, world has gripped under recession. It does not matter, how much regulations we put for data privacy or banking, the scams are kept on surfacing. Global warming is another menace, thirsty for blood. If that was not enough, artificial intelligence is another hazard that we expect to eat up all our jobs. Anti-social elements are using religious theories against the humanity whereas the basic foundation of religion is compassion. The cost of human life is nothing. Natural calamities are just another routine news for us.

Having discussed all this, we have 2 solutions,

1. Let's leave the world as it is, and expect that time and Nature will solve everything.
2. Another solution is, take control of the future and design it

Quite obvious, we have largely followed option 1 and we are on the verge of world war and global warming. So let's look at the option 2.

Now, for option 2 to work, we should know what is root cause problem of our world, then only we can focus on resolving the problem. We know all the more disciplines than past. But what we do not know is, how to use them or where is the problem. It is a perfect case of catch 22 situation. Let's look at some of the major problems:

- How to contribute to global warming, should I stop my nation's development
- How can I avoid world war, if I stop stockpiling nuclear war fares, am I not risking my nation's security?

- How can I prevent future job losses, if I do not work on developing my technology, somebody else will do it and I will lose the edge?

Unknown:

Let just pause for a moment, what future we are leaving for next generations. A world full of sorrow, hatred, struggle, war, depleted natural resources etc. when do we really wake up to feel that world and nature needs us otherwise it will go in irreversible status. We have to make conscious and serious effort towards it.

Let's understand with this analogous problem, a village is having flood every alternative month. One way is to build tolerant houses, arrange doctors for treatment, lawyers for dispute and so on. While the other solution is, to look at the reason why flood is happening. While former was the short term solution (and to some extent necessary) but certainly, we need long term solutions for the problem.

Let's look at the world with a different perspective, when we talk of developed countries, we talk about number of citizens against each doctor, lawyer, policeman etc. rather why do not we strive to create a world where there is no need of doctors, lawyer, policemen. Because these professions exist when there is a problem of some kind. What is the point of having a reactive and passive approach of increasing doctors, lawyers? Why not to work towards health and human behavior to treat the disease itself. We all agree that kind of problems that we have today, cannot be treated in isolation.

can we imagine a world, where people treat each other as a part of one big family, with brotherhood, love and affection, where we all belong to single set of values (irrespective of our birth place, color of the skin, age, caste etc.), a world where values are more important than physical possessions, people like to follow rules not because there is a policeman and court? If you believe the above section was figment of my imagination, next section is mandatory for you.

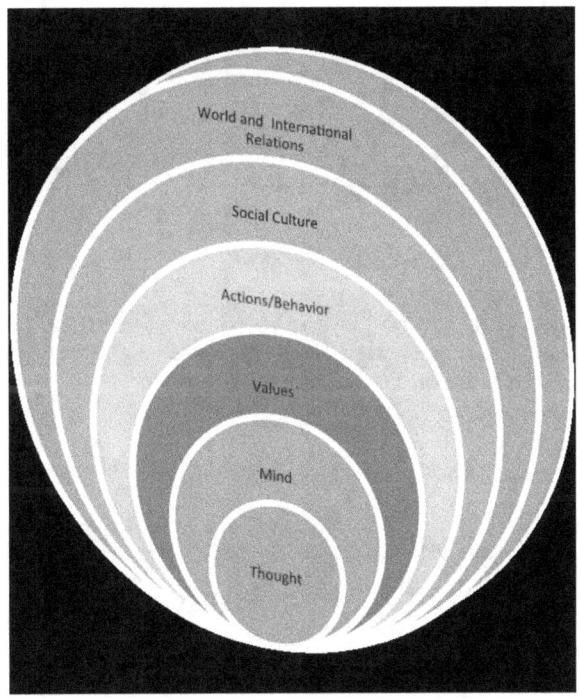

Process of Transformation

The future state might look difficult or impossible but unfortunately, we are out of options and this is the only play left.

So how to get out of this catch 22 situation, there has to be a holistic approach which should cater all problems at once. Today, we almost know everything about nature, and science but what we do not know is the purpose of our life (the root). The long awaited question of Who am I and what is my purpose are the prime mysteries to resolve. For this approach, let's study the most basic fundamental unit of universe "Thought". If we can catch hold of this unit, we can resolve every aspect of human behavior. If you closely look at the all the above problems, they are directly linked to human behavior.

If we want to design a new future and study the dynamics of thoughts, we have to answer below 2 questions first,

I. Who am I (the owner of thoughts)
II. Natural and Moral Laws

Journey to find Who am I, is an inter-disciplinary approach and difficult to cover in this short section. Long story short, before we start the journey, let's look into the few laws that applies to thoughts:

Law 1

Let's start with a mind power exercise, mark your watch and hold just one 'seed thought' (Seed thought is nothing just the initial root thought) in your mind, i.e. "You are in middle of the amazon jungle" for 60 seconds………………………………………………………………..

Now, wherever I have done this exercise to my training group. People used to say their experience something like below:

I saw wild creatures, snakes are sneaking in, tigers are roaring. How I will get out or what a scenic beauty etc. I am sure you must have had your version as well where you could describe it in different words and number of sentences.

I love to tell you did not followed instructions correctly. Instruction was to stay tune to single 'seed thought' only, I never said about trees, creatures. You built it yourself (if you wish to try again, try it one more time). But do not worry, you have just experienced the law of evolution.

Law of evolution simply says, Thoughts are dynamic in nature. They operate in chain reaction, i.e. one thought giving rise to several other thoughts in continuation. It is like throwing a stone in the pond, it will create ripple waves.

Similarly, when you create a thought, ripples start floating automatically in a dialectical way.

Just like in physics, you start with Newton's 3rd law and goes on to derive super complex formulas. Which is the very basis of theory of evolution. Extrapolating this law of evolution means, once you generate single thought (i.e. Seed thought), it will create another thought as a product/ripple and will go on. Like in the above exercise, you started with one thought that "I am in jungle", followed up by, "wow, there is no traffic or pollution", "There could be dangerous creatures",

"I should not stay here long", "What about my family" etc. the figure shows the different thoughts coming out of seed thought (which is the middle). Follow-up thoughts are shown in bullets format.

Law 2

Let's do another mind power exercise, think of the happiest moment of your life.

For example,

- when you met your crush for the first time,
- how you used to play with your pet,
- how you felt upon receiving the most prestigious award.
- Your kid asking innocent questions
- etc

with these thoughts in your mind, how are you feeling at this point of time? If you look yourself into mirror, you would see a smiling face, relaxed, confident etc. it would not be wrong to say that your energy level has gained. You can choose to invest your energy.

On the contrary, if I ask you to dwell into passive thoughts: such as

- the last embarrassing discussion you had with your boss
- or the Most embarrassing moment of your life

- how you felt when you failed miserably and became hopeless
- etc

if you have spent good enough time absorbing above thoughts. what has changed in your energy level? Shoulders are down, chin is facing chest and energy level is down. With this state of mind, you may have physical strength but mental energy is absent.

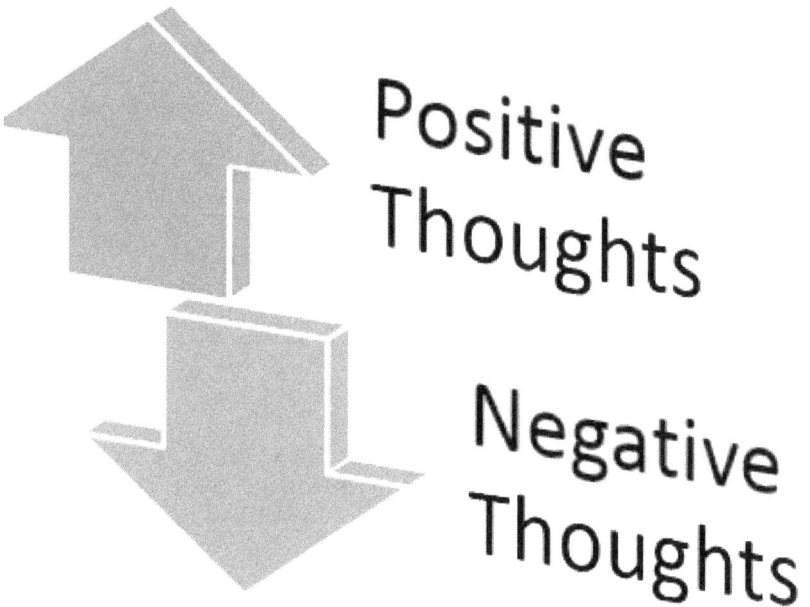

Conclusion to the above exercise, thought is a form of action wherein we first invest our energy and as a byproduct, we are either gaining or losing energy. So our intent should be to generate thoughts which have better ROI (return on investments = investment/Return).

Law is every thought is either producing energy or consuming energy.

Combining above 2 laws. Can we find out Unique Positive Seed Thought which has a property of radiating only positive thoughts and positive energies. In the following chapters, the mystery of a brilliant seed thought will be revealed along with its impact on organizational culture.

Chapter 3.2

Training Module 2: Application of Meditation

Importance of UPST (Unique Positive Seed Thought) and its Fundamentals

Before we implement the concept of Seed thought to our Businesses, let's look at its importance at macro level.

Rationally, if we look at the school of thought of Terrorism, it is an achievement to attune someone's mind to the extent that he or she should be ready to sacrifice his life. People are doing it so they are successful.

The very genesis of Terrorism came from Darwin's theory. It says, monkeys/apes are our ancestors. Human is an evolved form of animals. This is a dangerous ploy,

- if I am just an animal, my basic instinct to hunt for food.
- There are only 2 types of people who are famous, either too good or too bad. For being good, serve society and tolerate all the politics, resistance and that too for the years (i.e. Mother Teresa spent her life). The other way is, do something evil so people should remember you, i.e. killing people for sport

- In jungle, when tiger is hunting a deer, it is survival for tiger and sin for deer. So you cannot say whether this act is good or bad. It is all about perspective, whether you are following Deer or Tiger. So the definition of right and wrong doings does not exist. Hence, Ethical and moral values are not mandate rather mere recommendations.
- Death is nothing but a reset button, even newton's 3rd law (i.e. every action has an equal and opposite reaction) does not apply here. if you kill 100 or 1000 people, the punishment is same for a suicide bomber. This is a failure of Newton's 3rd law, how can killing 1 person and 100 people massacre is having same punishment.

Seed Thought: Human is an animal

Moral & Ethical actions are no mandate

It's a Jungle rule, hunt or hunted

Nothing is wrong or Right, just a matter of perspective

Death: a Reset to zero

Moreover, Death resetting to zero is also not a valid concept, it does not follow the very law of nature or Newton's law, i.e. what you sow, so shall you reap. Terrorist killing 1 people and 1000 people with suicidal bomb is getting same treatment (death) then it is a complete violation of Newton's 3rd law. This is the primary reason why humanity has failed and terrorism surfaced. If you could notice that we have just justified Terrorism using the Darwin's theory as seed thought.

Same applies to our organizations as well, every business thought or value has a power to make or break any organization. An organizational value has an everlasting impact on organizational culture and its employees, which actually decide the very fate of our business. For a thought to succeed, it needs to follow a dialectical approach to reach goal, then only it will form a bond with emotions.

For example, if you start a campaign to ask your people to do extra work or generate more sales, your seed thought should be good enough to explain why is it needed and attach a positive emotion to it.

You should be able to foresee (to 3rd or 4th generation) what people are going to infer out of it, whether these inferred thoughts are aligned with my business objective or not. Seed thought should be so much powerful that all of its byproduct thoughts produce positive energies.

How many times do we witness, management is focusing on an issue and resolution which lower management either not aware of or not understand the gravity of it? As a result, there is a great vacuum between the senior leadership and lower management. This approach is very important is driving a designed corporate culture and then controlling it.

Journey to Universal Positive Seed Thought (UPST)

As we have seen above that every seed thought releases series of thoughts (Produced thoughts) along with their respective energies. In this chapter. You are going to witness the seed thought which has the power to change the course of our world.

In this journey to explore the UPST, Let's start with an example, take another social abuse, i.e. Rape.

Why do people rape, what is their current seed thought that they are working on, if you were to replace that what would be the new thought, etc?

In my opinion, below is the thought tree should be happening in his mind. They would first feel the craving for the lust and consider it as a physical need. Then they will feel the fun part of it. And eventually they decide that this is worth trying for. Let's take a chance to dodge legal systems.

Now, there are 2 options to stop rapes. Either you formulate law such that each and every thought (in thought tree) is controlled or eliminated with the fear of law. Second option is change the seed thought itself.

If you follow the former approach, you will continuously be making & amending laws, and criminals will keep on finding the loop holes in that. So I follow the second approach.

Let's get into the details of thought "I am a body". Whether it is a truth or not?

When I say, I am body, what are the specificities, because I also has values, beliefs, personality traits (that's what we are trying to focus), skills, etc.

Is it brain, heart or something else. On the contrary, why we always say, this is my brain, is my heart beating correct, I can't see through my eyes, I can't hear etc. this means we are user or controller of these organs and different from physical body. That would also mean that my body may have its needs but I being a separate entity may have different needs, e.g. Love, affection, respect etc. I may have full stomach, but if everybody hates me then I may not be enjoying my life very well.

Henceforth, it is clearly evident that we are different from our bodies and we are using these organs. Then the next question would be, if I am not body then who I am?

The fact is, we all are eternal and perpetual source of energies, we may call it "Soul" for referencing purposes. Soul is eternal because energy can neither be created nor destroyed. Soul is capable of creating thoughts. it is these thoughts that translates into actions. Soul is sitting in your forehead and controlling your whole body. When we hit our feet, millions of neurons communicate this message to soul. Just like a driver driving a car. It remains seated at one place and control the whole mechanism.

Let's follow a statistical approach. Assume that we all are bodies, piece of flesh and blood (null hypothesis) and see to what extent this null hypothesis holds true:

- Why twin babies have different personalities amidst grown in same environment: this is the most basic question in the field of psychology, which it fails to answer. One of the answer it has, during the process of reproduction, several male sperm count reach out to female egg. Now depending upon the which sperm count reaches first, the personalities and other traits of Individual are interpreted. Now if I ask, what is the science behind mating of sperm-egg. People says, it is a matter of chance which is a polite way of saying that we do not know. As we have already seen above, the moment we consider ourselves bodies or creatures, it has a hazardous effect on our society.

The second generation of this school of thought would also presume that physical disabled babies are unlucky who don't get the healthy mating process. This also means that Nature and GOD does not have any adequate laws. So Nature and GOD by its very inheritance are law breakers or in another words biased. Being part of nature, we are allowed to be biased. If not, we are against natural laws. So it is clearly evident, following above methodologies, we are actually giving a life a new devil.

On the other hand, we cannot undermine the fact that whole universe and nature is operating under the laws of science and physics. How come this process does not fall under this category. It is clearly evident that we are missing something.

Null hypothesis rejected.

- Why some infants are born with golden spoon in the mouth and others are excruciating poverty: there are kids who are born in royal families, does not know what hunger is, they have raised under super pampered environment. Whereas the other kid is raised in Sahara Desert, where even the basic facilities (like water) are not there. Since his childhood, he has only seen adversities of hunger, pain etc. The basic law of civilization, that person should only get punished when he has done something wrong. On what basis, GOD or Nature (whosoever) is punishing them, what is the basic underlying factor which makes them deserve this adversity.

Null hypothesis rejected.

- Why some people are born musician or artist: if we all are just pool of bodies, how come some people are born talented. Few kids play music instruments so fluently and rhythmically that they can beat the best of the masters of music. Other are blessed with dancing, scientific experiments they almost have no learning curve. How come their learning curve is so small as compared to other individuals? Merely saying, they are GOD gifted does not solve anything nor it is a scientific explanation. Null hypothesis rejected.

- Brain transplantation change personality: Since beginning of this book, we are talking about thoughts, and transforming personality. Obvious fact is, Thoughts are created in Brain that would also mean our personality traits, belief are also somewhere in brain. In that case, brain transplantation should change the complete personality which do not happen so that means we do not know where does thoughts, personality traits reside. Null hypothesis rejected.

- Newton's 3rd law: newton's 3rd law is the basis of complete science. Without this law, we can't even walk on earth. So how come, this law is not applicable to overall life cycle. Coming back to terrorism example, why the terrorists are not punished as per their evils. Why nature spare them.

- Past life regression therapy: in this therapy, it is to be believed that whatever disease we have today, is linked to our previous lives. In this therapy, doctors try and surface the previous life incidents and then explore the appropriate medication. If we all flesh and live only once, then how come this theory even exists. Which entity has taken re-births, is it body or something else? Null hypothesis rejected.

In the light of the above hypothesis testing, it can be concluded that we are different from bodies and carry some impressions from previous birth. Since, the physical body is destroyed (e.g. cremated etc) then it can only be energy that gets another body.

So the conclusion is: "I am a soul and carry impressions in next birth (good deeds or bad deeds)". The UPST would be "I am a GOD's gifted creation bounded with law of Karma".

Let's see the above examples of Terrorism and Rape with this seed thought.

New thought for Rapist:

New Thought for Terrorist:

If a rapist would know that I am actually a soul (not a body), I am a master of these intellectual (thoughts and mind) & physical faculties (organs), then I have the power to control these. Moreover, law of karma always prevails, it does not matter, if the legal system is able to prove you guilty or not. The Karma will make sure you get what you deserve so there is no escaping. Restlessness is in my soul, created by my thoughts, lust is temporary arrangement, it is like, burning your leg to get warm in cold winter.

Remember, every action/behavior/process starts with a thought, once this input is ready, our mind (not brain which is physical) works like a filter and decides which thought is good enough for action. Once a thought passes mind, releases respective emotions and the soul becomes the embodiment of the that thought or emotion. This is a complete cycle, once a thought is actioned, it forms a value or leave impression on the soul which becomes the source of origination of thought.

For example, if you have not eaten sweet in your life, you have a thought of trying it. Mind gives its approval; you happen to eat it. As a result of which you enjoy the taste of sweetness. this sweetness leaves an impression on your soul and next time when you see the sweet, thought of previous experience will emerge again and will trigger the thought again. Thoughts also gets their feed form the impressions, environment, values etc.

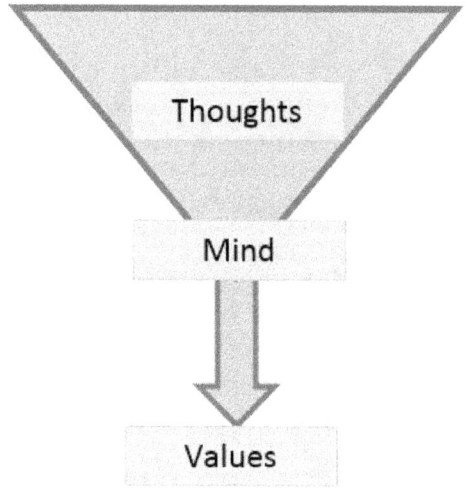

Having understood this concept, every soul has limited energy. So it is up to you where do you want to invest it. Remember, every thought is either consuming or releasing energy so it is an action.

There are few innate abilities of the soul:

- Universe has a tendency to achieve lowest energy state which we call stable state. Its explanation involves the concept of physics (i.e. entropy and kinetic & potential energies) so I want to avoid at this point of time. Soul is no different, in native state is peaceful and it is the state of lowest energy. No matter how much music and other things you enjoy. At the end of the day, you would want peace and serenity. Just like in nature, every element wants to achieve a state of stability,

- Soul wants to love and be loved so always a well-wisher. Deep inside, it defines your purpose of life and gives you satisfaction. The general belief spread my media and researchers that world is difficult place to live, people always wants to take advantage of you are negative ecosystems. These belief systems negatively influence the values of the soul and thereby thought pattern. On the contrary, soul (by design) always wants to have harmony because it gives rise to positive emotion that you are valued.

- Soul, by nature is confident. You watch small kids. They will do things without thinking of failure. Weak self-confidence is like an infection or disease. It is because of low self-esteem and inaccurate belief systems.

As per my opinion, it is all part of karma. Every weakness or strength (be it mental or physical) is a result of your actions. When we perform any action, we are bound to reap its repercussions. We might have rest of the world convinced that our unpleasant action was justified but we can't lie to our own self. Soul by its very nature knows what is right. For example, some people believe that eating non-veg is good for earth ecological balance and it is nutritious as well, they will be able to prove it statistically that it is the only option the planet earth has. But if you ask them to dissect the creature by themselves or witness the whole process in front of their eyes. 50% of them will not be able to face. Because deep down they all know that it is not right. It creates a conflict within their minds.

Law: whenever you are going against the laws of nature (i.e. kindness etc), you are bound to have conflicts within yourself. Today, you might have the power to subside it but it takes your energy and settle down at bottom.

7 Virtues of the Soul

We are what we need the most.

- Peace
- Love
- Happiness
- Knowledge
- Power
- Purity
- Bliss

- Soul finds a way to happiness and bliss, it is the thoughts that give bliss to soul. Any material goods in itself are not capable of resonating happiness, it is our attitude toward that material makes us happy. Same applies to the adverse circumstances, they are adverse because they are beyond our narrow horizon. It is our reactions that makes us weak. If we can remain our calm and composure, then there will no turbulence.

- Satisfaction is in mind, not in the outside world. You might have seen people who are happy what they have (despite the fact they have little of everything) then there are people who own kingdom and still unsatisfied. Physical bodies do not provide any satisfaction or dissatisfaction on their own, it depends upon the mindset of the user, how he takes it. That is the precise reason why some people are happy by just watching birds and jungles whereas others are finding faults in Niagara Falls and dissatisfied. Whenever a thought is generated, it yields a deep emotion associated with it. For example, when you see raining, if you have a thought, "oh my God, how I am going to office, it is going to be huge traffic jam, so irritating". This thought will generate a feeling of irritation (because you chose it so). On the other hand, if you think, "it is going to be a wonderful day, weather temperature is going to come down, maybe we can go out for a picnic." These thoughts will yield a positive emotion of rejoice so you will be satisfied with the weather.

- Soul in its nature has all the above mentioned virtues, it is the wild attractions/detractions that makes us weak. In simple words, every soul is full of positivity and expert in certain subject. It is the mindset and subtle weaknesses that is stopping us. Details are going to be covered in the chapter of positive Self talk.
- You wonder what is the difference between a successful and failure

celebrities. It is nothing else but the thoughts.

Law: If you can control your thoughts, you can control your world

1st step of meditation is self-realization, that means we visualize our self as soul, an entity different from body, the owner of complete system (subtle powers and physical body). As the realization deepens, the above mentioned qualities start surfacing, automatically.

In the second stage, the soul connect itself to the supreme power house. For that connection to be established, there are certain characteristics, we should know about GOD. And these are universal in nature so it does not matter, what religion you believe in,

- GOD is the creator; he is also a point of light just like soul.
- GOD is an ocean of love, that means he does not get mad, if you have done sins in the past.
- Rather he is Merciful and ready to forgive all your bad acts
- GOD is power house of all the energies and virtues
- GOD is our father of all of our souls, he loves you for the fact that he is our father

Let's begin with the process of Meditation, ground rule is, Soul can only connect with him, if you are elevated. I am a weak soul, please forgive me my sins, will only resonate an emotion that you are a weak soul. Rather, you should teach yourself that you are a powerful soul means positive healthy emotions.

Meditation is a process of self-healing and learning where we condition our mind towards positivity. The complete process of Meditation is explained below:

Inculcate below thoughts in a closed room with no disturbance, you can play slow instrumental music with comfortable clothes. Try and slow down the frequency of thoughts. For any thoughts of distraction, don't cut them, just let them pass by, and recall that you are elevating yourself.

"I am a soul, sitting in the forehead, I am driving this body, I am the energy and owner of all subtle and physical faculties (e.g. thoughts, mind, brain, eyes etc). I am a peaceful soul. All my thoughts are getting peaceful.my physical body is getting covered with rays of peace. I the soul, is shining like a brilliant star and spreading light in the room. All of the material things are getting enlightened.

My father is a supreme soul. We have a relationship of father and son. He is my lovable father, an ocean of peace and love. My father always stays in a peaceful state. Does not change ever. He is washing away my bad values and I am feeling light. I am transforming into a peace messenger and my only duty is to spread peace in to the world"

If you practice above thoughts, you will garner peace as the thoughts only related to peace. This was just the small example what we could do if we alter the input (i.e. Thoughts).

A business owner can manifest loyalty, increase job satisfaction etc within your employees. Enterprise level initiatives are presented in upcoming chapters.

Meditation refreshes RAM and ROM memory of our mind so that we could channelize our energy. In second step of meditation, the soul realization experience is taken to next level by connecting it the supreme power house, the GOD. Soul weaknesses are like mouse trap; it need somebody to open the cage. Meditation is that help.

These concepts will be used extensively in the coming chapters of this book. you will witness a lot of examples and research studies from various disciplines. Benchmarking is always a great concept in business consulting, this book is no different, I have taken learnings from the various industries (Corporates, MNCs, Spiritual Organizations, NGO, Science, Defense forces etc). to make our corporate world more efficient. This theory goes down to nucleus of the problem and then talks about the ways for resolution. since this being a vast topic, my approach is precisely focused.

Moreover, Meditation is not something new, we all are doing it knowingly or unknowingly. We all condition our mind form the time we get up in the morning, till we sleep. It is just a conscious effort to plant a certain seed into employee's mind.

Chapter 4

Defining and Measuring the Extent of Hazards of Poor Culture

The theory is pragmatic approach of measuring and leveraging the most valuable asset of the organization (i.e. Employee's thought) by institutionalizing the concept of Meditation. Theory follows a tops to bottom approach and idealize an organization environment where employee love to come to office than home to the extent he is ready to work for free if situations calls for it thus helping business creating a niche advantage.

Like in other process improvement techniques (e.g. Lean, Six Sigma, etc), we often read about standardization of work, in this approach, we focus on standardization of thoughts, so that employer and employees think alike and should be in synch.

Question: On Sunday 6:00 PM, you are looking forward to a good family time or equivalent leisure and you receive a call that your services are needed, can you please help? Considering the fact that you will not be paid and this will not have any future repercussions (especially if you say NO, in case of office) be it good or bad.

Prioritize your list as to where you would want to go happily:

- Office or work place
- School, College or Educational institution
- Your Religious place (where you believe)

When I have asked this question and Office was generally the last option (means people will not like to go to office on Sunday evening if it is not paid). Even few people asked me, why they even calling me on Sunday, don't they know it is my off.

Now as a CEO, it disappointment me, because office is the only place where you actually earn money rest all others are expenditure. Then why do people always measure or correlate their work stations primarily with money.

This does not end here, all type of work in corporates can be divided into 2 categories, i.e. Mechanical and intellectual. Monetary benefits are good catalyst for boosting mechanical productivity. For intellectual activities (involves creativity and innovation), monetary benefits are distraction. Have you ever wondered why some of the old classic songs (e.g. from Kishore Kumar era) were so melodious and why modern music lacks creativity? Because old sings were made out of passion less of earning money. Increase in wages does not guarantee that you are completely leveraging their installed intellectual asset. In other words, paying high salaries is not a solution. There is only one way to leverage intellectual assets that is improve culture. Let's start a project with this context.

Defining the Problem

- How to leverage employee's intellectual asset of the employees?
- Secondary metric would be, increase the number of positive thoughts about organization per employee per hour.
- Goal: to bring the organization in Black hole in pyramid of transformation. Thereby improve employee retention%, increase efficiency, less change resistance, manifest loyalty etc.

Strategic execution is accomplished through inclusion and getting a culture that not only understands your strategy and direction, but has the ability to break through silos and work together – subjugating personal goals for a higher purpose. Building a culture grounded in really smart communication additionally becomes a strategic recruiting weapon for your organization and enables the smartest and best people to develop. This happens through clear messaging and accountability. The role that leadership plays in strategic execution is enormous. Aligning around a clear set of deliverables and holding people accountable is key.

To be in Black Hole of Pyramid of Transformation, we need to ask few questions, has your organization embraced your vision, mission, core values and value proposition? Getting the right foundations in place and then ensuring that both words and actions align is difficult.

When organizations lack common language and understand and there is a poor rhythm of communication and messaging through the organization, it becomes impossible create momentum, engagement and focus.

Measure the extent of problem:

Kodak: In 1998, Kodak stores were almost at every corner of globe and the company had around 180,000 employees. The company was leading the photography world and was a huge success. Its technological edge was good enough to mark it as a market leader, it could produce digital cameras and was one of the first companies to know how to do so, it didn't build on the idea because it didn't want to compete with its own traditional film business. In short, the company didn't want to innovate and ready to take the risk. Instead, Kodak sat back as other companies eventually came out with the technology that essentially took down its core business. Instead of capitalizing on new technology and innovative change, Kodak was focused on only the next quarter and showed some fear for the future when it should have been thinking about the possible long-term gains.

Similar examples, are seen every day at companies around the world. Instead of focusing on innovation/change and where the company can be in the future, companies often get tangled in culture of politics. When employees, especially managers/dept heads, are more concerned about keeping their jobs and moving up in the company, a culture that squanders innovation is born. It is a very common practice, whenever any new VP or Head joins, he/she bring some radical changes so as to highlight his/her visibility. The primary motive is get limelight and secondary to benefit production or organization. Low grade employees that are the most passionate about change and innovation can be silenced until they burn out or quit because they face so many obstacles to make change happen. It can be disheartening to be a forward-thinking employee at a company so firmly rooted in its current state.

In today's tech-powered world, innovation happens at an astronomical pace, and having a culture that doesn't support that growth can significantly hurt your company.

In nutshell,

- In the light of recent changes in the world, it can be said that if employees are not aligned with organizational goals then business will lose the competitive edge and may not able to cope up with the turbulent scenarios.
- Negative politics and hostile culture can harshly damage the ability of an organization to cope up change and flourish.

---------------------Part 3---------------------
DEPLOYING THEORY OF ZERO SALARY

Chapter 5. Planting a solution

Chapter 5

Planting a Solution

Currently employees believe that organization is profit oriented and has nothing or little to do it with employees (it can shell out employees if needed). This belief system is hazardous to company. Employees will only perform to an extent to save his job or when his own promotion is due. In either of the case, he will not consider organizational objective. More we grow with this belief, deeper we go into trouble. Our project is to align employee's thought with company's objectives by establishing an emotional bond with organization.

In our project, the metric we are going to use is, the number of thoughts per employee per hour that support above notion is greater as compared to thoughts oppose above notion.

Secondly, the organization has impacted only outer part of the brain (by monetary benefits), not the inner part of the brain which actually deals in emotions.

Please look into these examples who were able to develop beneficial culture with zero salary or expenses along with their business dynamics.

Phase 1

Would you like to join an organization having employee base of 2 million and widely respected for their team culture and loyalty. The training is done under strict discipline with absolutely zero tolerance for mistakes. The schedule is tough and leaves little time for rest. Strict punishments are just a part of daily routine.

You might have guessed till now, it is the Armed Forces. Soldiers aren't just fighting the enemies. They're also fighting natural disasters. At such high altitudes, frost bites, chilblains, loss of memory and pulmonary edemas are common problems. Bonus part is, dealing with avalanches and crevasses along with the threat of enemy attacks at any given time.

Amidst the low monetary benefits, the team culture is at its peak. Team culture is so much perfect that it can cost lives of the team members.

It is perfect case study to learn the concepts of Team culture.

Phase 2

In the context of organization culture and monetary benefits, let me raise this bar furthermore, in the previous case, employees are still getting monetary rewards. There are organizations, wherein people don't get to paid anything. And still they work better than the paid professionals. Furthermore, the paid professionals may have health issues but these free professionals are very happy. Employee satisfaction is supreme in this case.

These organizations are nothing but spiritual organizations. Theory of zero salary says that build your organizational culture such that employee should be willing to work for you free (ideal case) or with minimal salary. There is also one profit making organization who has implemented part of this theory and their business model is so niche that it can't be replicated. No other organization is able to replicate or match its standards. It is no other Mumbai Dabba Wala. They have a flat salary and people come and join this organization. They don't resign, only retire. This is the power of theory of zero salary. The employees are not given any additional facilities, and team takes pride working with Mumbai Dabba Wala.

Question is how do I bring this culture into my organization.

The anatomy of organizational culture is shown below, every individual follow these circles and culture is formed at the outermost circle. Most effective and economical way to change the culture is, by impacting the thoughts of employees and stopping it from draining.

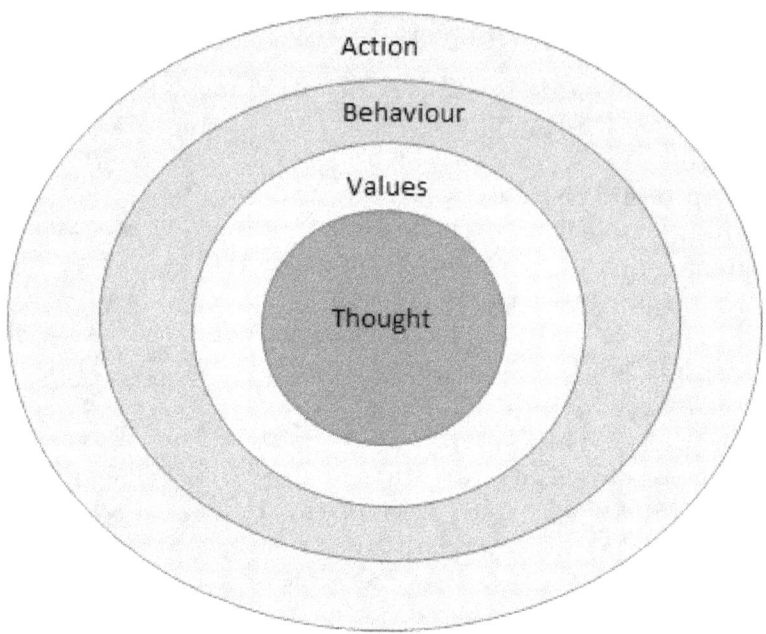

In the following chapters, we will focus on how to impact the thinking pattern of the employees at an enterprise level. Values are belief, type of thinking pattern or the way one perceives outer world (in our case company policies, environment, work profile and its colleagues etc). Employee's thoughts are the input to nuclear chain reaction of culture. It has exponential effect on overall culture of the organization. Single positive unit of employee thought will create multiple units of positive culture, same is true for other side as well. Companies like Microsoft, Google, Infosys invest so much in building culture and employee retention because it is solely responsible for organizational growth.

As long as we are living being, we are constantly thinking (even when we are sleeping). the process of transforming thoughts to Values are defined below: firstly, we have all types of thoughts, for example,

- I should work hard so that I will get the promotion in my career, etc.

- Why do I have to work hard, I am going to get the same salary or the additional bonus is not much,

- If I work too much, my manager will give me more work

Basis on his/her belief system which is based on his experience with previous companies/Managers or company culture or personal experience etc), he will select any of the above thought. This will result in his action and form his values. In the following chapters, we will be focusing on impacting the thoughts pattern of the employees thereby removing the personal conflicts and manifesting loyalty.

Chapter 5.1

Cultural Fit

Resigned employees are long term cost which often gets ignored. Process of retaining employees starts from Hiring, factoring in the concepts of shared values and cultural beliefs leads to winning results. And I'd argue that culture fit is the most important aspect of retaining great employees above anything else. It becomes all the more important as macro-economic factors are facing significant changes. But employee retention starts with first being able to clearly articulate what the organizational culture is. What are the aligned values, beliefs, behaviors and experiences that make up the organization's environment?

[3] Defining company culture and values can be done in several ways. But it must be done. Whether senior leaders are working with consultants or working together as a committee, company culture and values should be observed on paper, including personal and professional aspects. Those involved must truly be aligned on what the best culture is that fits the ultimate vision of the organization. I repeat, the culture should align with achieving the vision and goals of the company. If the existing culture needs some changes, then so be it.

Organizational culture comes about in one of two ways. It's either decisively defined, nurtured and protected from the inception of the organization; or — more typically — it comes about haphazardly as a collective sum of the beliefs, experiences and behaviors of those on the team. In our project, we are advocating for former case. Just like we plan and control other business assets, culture should also be planned and controlled.

Once the company culture has been defined, ideally every action, strategy, decision and communication should support the cultural beliefs — including all HR mechanisms from recruitment and hiring processes to performance review systems.

Culture fit so important for recruiting and retaining great talent. New joiners that don't mesh well with the existing or desired company culture leads to poor work quality, decreased job satisfaction and a potentially toxic environment. This results in turnover which has high costs — both hard and soft.

On the other hand, hiring employees that fit well with the culture and share a strong belief in the values will most likely flourish. A great study on the subject revealed that employees who fit well with their organization, coworkers, and supervisor had greater job satisfaction, were more likely to remain with their organization, and showed superior job performance. This is especially important when the organization is facing the unavoidable changes, volatility and ambiguity it will experience many times throughout its lifecycle. A strong team with shared values is nimbler and can adapt more readily.

Have you ever doubted, why nobody else could match the standards of Mumbai Dabba Wala. You hire best of the talent from finest universities, still you will find it difficult to run such company. One it is the geographical map of Mumbai and second is cultural fit. They only hire people from one village. This is the prime reason of their success and what makes them unique. The variation of thoughts among the employees is tiniest. They all believe that they are working for good cause so their consciousness is high and consistent among all. Culturally, they also match each other. Negative politics is at the least. One more unique factor about them, when a person coming from village to join Mumbai Dabba Wala, it works with them for all his life, post which his son (next generation) will work. Imagine, how much aligned they are. When a new person is joining, he has legacy to carry. Since, the pay structure is also flat so there is no question of bonus pay or variable pay or promotion. So everybody is at ease.

As an organization, we can't hire only from one village to reduce the variation of thoughts. All of my proposals described in this book, are intended to reduce the variation of thoughts, values and cultures. If you aim to transform the personality of your employees towards positivity. You are doing good for them and for business. It can't be the case where the employees become positive but still talking negative for the organization. If you developing and grooming them for better, let their friends and family notice and it will again come back to you.

Be it employee or employer's perspective, I am not asking to change anything, just the shift of consciousness. Employer should partner employees in growth, show them trust. Build your structure such that if an employee is upset and talking bad about company then other workers should stop him.

Chapter 5.2

Milagro: Power of Consciousness

Phase 1

Before we even talking about power of consciousness, let me show you the power of consciousness.

<u>Case 1</u>:

[4]Dashrath Manjhi worked on the other side of the mountain. At noon, his wife Phaguni would bring his lunch. As they had no road, the trek took hours over the mountain. Dashrath tilled fields for a landlord on the other side. He would quarry stone. And in a few hours from then, he would be tired and hungry.

Phaguni, Dashrath's wife, prepared for her treacherous climb up the mountain. She wrapped the 'rotis', filled a container with a thin curry, and bundled the food into a square of cloth. She picked a small pot of water, and hoisted it on her head. Her children sat playing by their hut in the small Musahar settlement in the mountain's shadow.

He would watch and wait for Phaguni. That day, she would come to him empty handed, injured. As the harsh sun beat down, Phaguni tripped on loose rock, and was badly injured. Her water pot shattered. She slid down several feet, injuring her leg. Hours past noon, she limped to her husband. He was angry at her for being late. But on seeing her tears, he made a decision.

He decided that he was not going to wait for anyone to solve his problems, he was going to do-it-himself.

He carved a path 110 m long (360 ft), 9.1 m (30 ft) wide and 7.6 m (25 ft) deep through a hillock using only a hammer and chisel. It took him 22 years of work, Dashrath shortened travel between the Atri and Wazirganj blocks of Gaya town from 55 km to 15 km.

Case 2:

The South Africa cricket team have become known as perennial chokers in major tournaments having lost all nine of their knockout matches in International Cricket Council tournaments over the past 15 years.

Britain is no stranger to the choke. Reading the newspapers, or overhearing pub conversations, you might well imagine it's a national pastime. The England football team? Ach, we'll crack up when it comes to penalties.

There's Jimmy White, who lost six snooker world championship finals and failed to pot a simple black to secure victory against Stephen Hendry in 1994; Jana Novotna, 4-1 up in the final set against

Steffi Graf, double-faulting her way to defeat and weeping on the shoulder of the Duchess of Kent in 1993; French golfer Jean Van de Velde who could have made a double bogey in the British Open at the 18th in 1999 and still won — but failed. The picture of Van de Velde paddling knee-deep in Barry Burn, trying to hit his ball out of the water, is one of sport's most comic and desperate images.

Above we have seen two shades of consciousness, it can make or break you. can you doubt on ability of all the celebrities mentioned in case 2 whereas Dashrath Manjhi would have had told you earlier that I will break this mountain? You would have laughed.

What is the consciousness? It is the picture of your own self in your mind. Consider yourself a depressing loser or performing hero, you will always be right. Question is, how can we turn it into Gold?

Irony is, you can't lie to yourself. Your honesty, purpose, inspiration, Self-respect will define your consciousness. Consciousness drives the values and behavior of the employees.

For higher consciousness, you should have clear goal of your career. Goal should be in terms of values and should have an inspirational figure to follow. See yourself as a valuable soul in its native state. There was a time, when the soul was free of all weaknesses and powerful in executing all his thoughts, capable of doing all activities that was required to perform. Be an epitome of perfection. No matter where you are and what you do, nobody can take away your past of innate abilities. Even if you find it difficult, fake it. There is a study which says that if you start faking, it will eventually become the reality.

I am a soul, master of body. I am the creator of my thoughts. I have the power to create my own world. My soul already has the inherent powers.

In the above cases, Dashrath Manjhi was deeply inspired and saw himself obligated to wife and society. Despite being financially poor, he has a great self-respect that if he has decided, he will complete it. In case 2, people had a doubt on their skills. In their minds, they portrayed themselves as loser and ultimately became.

Phase 2

Let me raise the bar. What do you think is the basic difference between the success and failures? It is the quality of thoughts. That means, for you to achieve any heights, just have to change the quality of thoughts. Your thoughts are your immune system, if you constantly experience negative emotions you will be subjected to stress and more sensitive to nerve-wracking situations. Being positive is the best defense against all the hassles, after all.

How good will be your survival and winning skills if you start your day with the food like "today I am going to use my complete potential and explore something new and do something extra ordinary".

What do you think, what difference it is going to make? when you first wake up in the morning, while doing meditation, you condition your mind that you are the most powerful soul in the world, and for rest of the day, you are going to help the needy (who are emotionally or psychologically weak) people. When people show anger or violent behavior, it is because they feel insecure from inside and they are weak. It takes great courage to combat adversities with calmness and very easy to lose control. It is not their fault because they have succumbed to the circumstances, they need somebody's help to pull them out of it.

If you try doing this exercise, you will find it difficult (even at times you will find it mundane and fake but do not give up, it is all part of learning phase) eventually, once you are through, it will become your muscle memory.

On the other side, coming to the business environment, we always deal so many different kinds of individuals, some of them are very smart, while others need help. What generally happens, you are a manager of a team and one of the member has done a big mistake which has dented your confidence in him. Now whenever you look at him, you consider him a looser, you don't say anything but it is evident from your actions. Now what is the consciousness that you are giving him (may be indirectly) that he is a looser and he is not capable of this role, etc. he will either go in depressing mode or think you never understood his case. And his performance is going to bottom rock. As you confront him again, your relationship will take a jog to a left. The radius of influence will keep on increasing between you and him. Because the root cause is, the consciousness that you are communicating is tearing apart his honor. He may be weak and looking for some emotional support from you, with this approach, he is only sinking in.

How to deploy it in an organization

Why not to celebrate each day of the week, organizations should complement it with screensavers, slogans and dress code's mandate, the success of these initiatives should be, people outside the organization should be able to see the difference,

- Monday as Day of happiness: we all know that Mondays are always difficult, no matter which industry you work for. Let there be a guideline that Monday is to celebrated as day of happiness. Start your official day with some light meditation music and everybody should have a thought that today I pledge to be happy and make others happy. I will forgive other mistakes (but make sure to highlight them in right spirit), just for today, I will keep a smile on my face. Every employee should act as a source of perpetual energy of happiness, the appreciation would be the consumer should be able to identify that today the company is celebrating happy day.

- Tuesday as day of Angel: on this day, all employees will have to consider themselves as angels, the idea is help any one employee is update it on the portal. The other employee should also acknowledge.

- Wednesday as day of calmness: every soul is calm and at ease. Any scolding and sarcasm are crime on this day, even if a person has done some error, you should show him the data, explain him the ramifications calmly (i.e. give direct feedback but politely). Negative talks are strictly prohibited.

- Thursday as day of sacrifice, every employee is a valuable asset and the organizational growth is only possible because of sacrifice made by their employees. Every employee is considered an epitome of sacrifice and dedication, every team has to celebrate, smallest of the sacrifices made by their team members. For example, if an employee has cancelled his leave and personal plans due to company urgencies.

- Friday as day of light: being carefree not careless. Soul is itself a light. So it is very easy for us to remain light in our thoughts. All employee should see each other as light. If any person is feeling heavy or stressed, all should help him.

These virtues are just indicative, please feel free to include some more.

Chapter 5.3

Renovatio

This concept says, that every day is a new birth of your team member, like we die and take rebirth. We don't remember from our past life. When a member is coming to office, make sure you give him a new day with new platform for challenges. You can learn from his past mistakes but don't let it hamper his today. Thought process for his bitter past is, "that was his bad day, let me try and explore what was the reason. Even if I think the reason is not well justified, let me give him another chance and I am hopeful that he is going to do well. Let me take this up as a challenge to nurture and groom him." Note, I am recommending you to follow this advice not because to make you a better person rather it has monetary benefit attached for organization.

Let me share a true example, one of my friend was working with ABC (not to disclose the name of the company), during the initial days of joining, one day he received an excel file to work. He got so nervous that could not do it and made it all wrong. His manager & AVP made fun of him, and gradually it became the usual practice. As long as his manager was there, he was an average performer. Then comes a day when his manager resigned, he took over the compete profile and promoted from Analyst to Manager which is a big leap considering the hierarchy of the company (the hierarchy was, Analyst to Sr Analyst to SME to Manager). How this guy suddenly became a star performer. Because earlier they were feeding his mind with negative consciousness. The idea is, never give up on your member, give him inspiration and show him the way. Feed him positive consciousness that he is a strong performer and has the capability to attain heights. You pass him ill consciousness, you are wasting money, loyalty, trust, pride, etc.

Insight: if a team is not performing as desired then it can be either skill (team members are skilled enough to perform the tasks) or WILL (members do not want to work) issue. For skill issue, it might be a hiring issue. If it is WILL issue, then it is time to deploy Renovatio. There is a high possibility that the manager's attitude is killing the motivation of the members. In case you think, your team member is of no use and he cannot contribute to company goals at all, your manager needs coaching. Moreover, this thought (that person is of no use) itself is not aligned with nature. Let's read the below study:

[7]The astonishing report, that the biomass of flying insects in Germany has dropped by three quarters since 1989, threatening an "ecological Armageddon", is the starkest warning yet; but it is only the latest in a series of studies which in the last five years have finally brought to public attention the real scale of the problem.

Does it matter? Even if bugs make you shudder? Oh yes. Insects are vital plant-pollinators and although most of our grain crops are pollinated by the wind, most of our fruit crops are insect-pollinated, as are the vast majority of our wild plants, from daisies to our most splendid wild flower, the rare and beautiful lady's slipper orchid.

Furthermore, insects form the base of thousands upon thousands of food chains, and their disappearance is a principal reason why Britain's farmland birds have more than halved in number since 1970. Some declines have been catastrophic: the grey partridge, whose chicks fed on the insects once abundant in cornfields, and the charming spotted flycatcher, a specialist predator of aerial insects, have both declined by more than 95%, while the red-backed shrike, which feeds on big beetles, became extinct in Britain in the 1990s.

Ecologically, catastrophe is the word for it.

What I am trying to say, each and every individual is equipped with some or the other skills. It is the job of a manager to find that skill and use it effectively. It does not matter, how much talent one has in his team, if manager is not capable, he will be a catalyst in killing skill and WILL of the people. You ask fish to climb tree and monkey to swim, you will end up in killing them both.

Even the insects that pest us are necessary for larger ecological balance and have their role to play. Every soul in this world has a definite role to play.

Consider the other person as soul (without gender) with special qualities. These qualities need your guidance to prosper. If he is not good in task A then try B, it is just a matter of doing the searching.

In nutshell, a manager or leader should be taught to compassionate with their fellow workers. It goes a long way.

Chapter 5.4

Sentido: Building Crystal Clear Thinking

This aspect is applicable to senior leadership and for the employees as well. Definition of Crystal clear thinking is keeping your thoughts (thus mind) focused which gives us the ability to connect dots and see the larger picture. This subsequently is a critical requirement for decision making. It is imperative for a leader to have crystal clear thinking because his decisions impact much larger audience and ripple effects are much stronger. Especially in today's world, the environment variables have increased so much. The growth of the organization depends upon the ability of its leader to comprehend number of variables at one point of time and see larger picture. Just one decision is good enough for rags to riches and vice a versa.

[5] Don Bradman had the greatest record and legacy of all batsmen. His footwork became legendary and influential for generations to come, but it was surely his mind and his ability to clear his thoughts away that was his greatest attribute. Bradman, there is no doubt, was misunderstood, especially by team-mates who stood shoulder to shoulder with him. They couldn't work out the mechanics of his mind, nor his beliefs and ability to perform beyond the norm, and some of them became envious of his record-breaking run-

making. Bradman was a private, single-minded man. He didn't drink, smoke, or socialize much during his playing days, unlike those he played with. He was different and he quickly became alienated due to his unexampled existence. In essence, no matter what the conditions, his thinking was sharp and focused: he saw the ball, reacted and moved accordingly, and that fearless mindset never left him. For one with no experience whatsoever in foreign conditions, it was a breathtaking performance.

Same applies to our business dealings as well, every decision could make or break revenue. Developing crystal clear thinking, it is an effort, it comes from practice and discipline of mind. What you think so shall you become. so there has to be a conscious effort to think only positive thoughts.

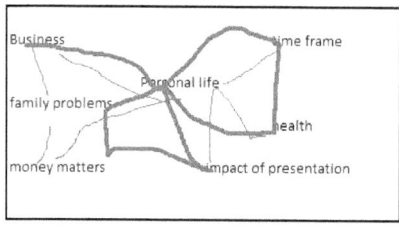

Confused State: Too Many Parameters

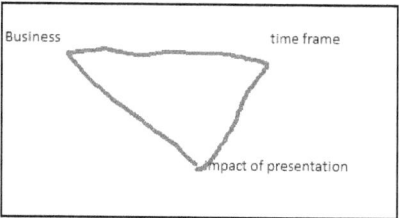

Clarity: Controlled Parameters

Currently, our mind is occupied with various thoughts, e.g. personal goals, relationship, professional politics etc. in simple worlds, there are attractions and detractions that continually amend or divert our focus. Right now, you may plan to read particular book, but mind is hovering somewhere else. Since we can't control our mind from going there, does not give us the concentration we want, hence no clarity in thinking.

The 1st thing that business calls for is Clarity, there are a lot of things that can (and frequently do) go wrong inside of a business. Sales fall through, products don't work, team members get frustrated, and clients get upset. While some of these scenarios play out as a result of outside surroundings, there's often another culprit to blame: lack of clarity.

In any reasonably complex organization, maintaining clarity in all things is of the utmost importance. Without it, organizations quickly come disjointed and little bumps—like an angry client or misinformed employee—turn into mountains. But with busy schedules, seemingly endless task-lists and diverse personnel, creating a smooth flow of communication can be a challenge. Usually no one is to blame but the process itself. But what can a business owner do to remedy a lack of clear communication?

Clarity is a habit and like any habit, it takes constant reinforcement. Here's the secret about clarity: it takes effort to achieve. There is no magic formula for ensuring that people are aligned and share a common understanding of the mission or task at hand. The only way to succeed is for all team members, regardless of rank or position, to make sure that clarity comes first in all exchanges.

It's the job of the leader to foster clarity, but success is still a team effort. If something isn't clear, it is still the responsibility of individual team members to speak up and try to fix the problem. Organizational clarity is a two-way street; everyone has to participate equally. The most important thing is to make the effort. If you manage to foster a culture of clarity inside of your organization, you'll see fewer problems, better execution, and happier, more productive teams.

Law: *Negativity or miscommunicating is costing either health or money to organization or society.*

All of our thoughts are pertaining to attraction or detractions (hatred). Attractions are possessions which we needed the most, detractions are items which we hate most. Our mind is constantly indulged either of them. These forces are responsible for lack of concentration and clarity. Clarity of mind is a muscle memory that needs to be developed with time. To be able to control inner most attractions and channeling energy in one direction is an art. That is where the concept of meditation comes in.

In Meditation, the first step is self-realization, as an experiment, try and realize the emotions coming out of below thoughts. sit in a comfortable position and clothing. If you encounter different thoughts, just witness them, don't cut those, let them pass by. Initially, you might have some difficulty in concentrating, it will come with practice.

To realize the emotions of peace, try below thoughts in serenity:

First step is to feel, that I am a source of peaceful energy: "I am a soul, energy who is driving this body. Peace is my native nature, by default I am a peaceful soul, etc"

Second step is to connect with supreme power (i.e. GOD).

One of the benefit of meditation is, it will withdraw your thoughts from all worldly subjects and refresh your mind and thoughts. Your RAM and ROM of your brain memory will be cleared and will be ready for use. Approximately, it takes 14 hrs of practice (2 hr per day) for an average individual to notice the differences. Keeping it very simple, we are a soul, and soul needs happiness, bliss and it will have it, no matter where you are and what you do. If you build your belief around the fact that bliss and happiness could only be found in the outer world or physical possessions, your mind will always be unruly. You will lose your concentration first. You will never be at ease because the world outside (including people) are so dynamic. And one of the thing that soul look for is security that you will not find anywhere as a result of constant wandering, either you will end up becoming negative personality or into depression. Because of the simple fact that you are dependent on the other people for your happiness and bliss who are themselves deprived and lost. Two lost passengers cannot guide each other.

Chapter 5.5

Serenidad: Non-Judgmental Attitude

Half knowledge is always dangerous. If you Jump to conclusions rather easily, making your mind usually before you hear all the facts, so you usually don't even listen to them.

You may be more judgmental than you realize. While no one necessarily likes to admit that they evaluate and label others, sometimes it happens so subconsciously that you don't even know you're doing it. Because judgments are ingrained so deeply in your subconscious, it can be hard to break the habit of immediately creating a label or generalization toward a person or situation.

For an organization to thrive, it is necessary that its managers should have non-judgmental attitude. 21st century is all about either change or die. Few examples of how companies are adapting, IBM has stayed relevant in different markets from hardware to software and has expanded its line of products, as well as its selling platform, dozens of times. Google and Facebook have been investing heavily in upcoming technologies like virtual reality, machine learning and artificial intelligence.

Some of the aspect of being non-judgmental:

1. Expanding your horizon

How many times have you stopped yourself from trying something new because you 'knew' you wouldn't like it? If you're like most people, the answer is probably a lot. However, if you set your judgment aside and try something new, you may find a pleasurable, exciting experience that enriches your life. Don't not try something just because someone else doesn't like it. There is a high possibility that your subordinate will come up with a new dimension and you are not even allowing him to speak or you listen to defeat him in the argument.

Being judgmental is like tightly holding a blade bare handed. It hurts you the most and then others. It shuts your brain to outside world. This attitude is a big problem for an Individual and to a company. Because it is the other way of manifesting frustration.

2. You have higher quality friendships

It's tough to be friends with someone who is always judging you. You feel like you're under the microscope with everything you do. This may cause you to only share information that you feel is 'safe' for discussion, often omitting personal and important parts of your life.

If, however, you're the type of friend who is non-judgmental, you tend to have higher quality relationships. Your friends know they can come to that you with personal information because you won't ridicule them for your actions or judge them for their not-so-good decisions.

They share more intimate life details because you've created a safe environment for them to do so. This means closer, higher quality friendships. This also affects your team management abilities. For a team member, being judgmental means that member should not open with you, if they do, you might use that as an excuse in appraisal meetings.

3. You achieve greater spirituality

When you free yourself from judging, you create a spirituality that is freeing. It's open to give and receive love on so many different levels. You feel calm and peace because you're not assigning labels or creating positives and negatives. Everything is seen for its own inherent beauty.

4. You are a happier person

When others are busy labeling things good, bad, right and wrong, you're just accepting them for what they are. And, when you're able to no longer judge things, you achieve a higher level of happiness because you're not weighted down by trying to figure out the complexities of people and situations. They are what they are. Nothing more. Nothing less.

And, when you're able to no longer label, you develop a stronger shield or thicker skin against those that live to label and judge. You are more resilient against getting sucked in to their negative thought patterns and behaviors.

How Do You Become Non-Judgmental?

The only way to correct it at root level is to meditate. Meditation changes your brainwaves (from beta to theta). What does this mean in layman terms?

When you're using beta brainwaves, which people in non-meditative states generally do, you are more susceptible to being nervous, stressed and depressed. With all of these negative emotions in your body, it's easy to cast a negative judgment on everything around you.

However, when your body switches to theta brainwaves, you feel more open and connected to other people. You are less judgmental of them, and have increased inspiration and motivation. Life becomes more positive.

There is a definite process we follow for being judgmental, when we sit for a discussion, we are already occupied in our thoughts and so much engrossed, the other person seems like shouting in chaos. Before, he could even begin, the mind start playing all the scenes from past, apprehensions, fear etc as a result of these mixed emotions, it becomes impossible to think clearly and understand the whole situation (it reduces your IQ).

How can you start to become non-judgmental today? Meditation increases the cortical thickness in the hippocampus, which runs the memory as well as the ability to learn new things. It helps with long term memory, which aids you with everything from giving a presentation to closing a sale to remembering your boss' husband's birthday. This part of the brain is also where Alzheimer's wreaks havoc, so a daily practice will do much more than assist you at the office. To get it started, find a nice, quiet place where you can sit and be alone. Close your eyes and focus only on your breathing. Then create below thoughts: "I am a peaceful soul, I order all my faculties to withdraw all its attention from the physical world. Let the frequency of thoughts slow down. Let the waste thoughts pass by because I am a peaceful soul, point of light. There was a time when I was powerful and free from all weakness, I could control my creation. Let me focus on my own self, how beautiful I am, such a sweet star." And so on. Once you dwell yourself into these thoughts, you will find a new loving personality.

By spending a few minutes every day performing this one little action, you'll be on your way to increased happiness, higher quality friendships and a new level of spirituality.

Chapter 5.6

Mindfulness: Deploying Meditation at an Organizational level

Phase 1

Buddhists have practiced mindfulness for more than 2,000 years, but West is finally waking up to the benefits of Eastern meditation and schools are discovering a daily dose of silent reflection can not only calm a classroom but may improve academic performance.

In recent years, medical science has discovered the extent to which mindfulness can help treat a range of mental conditions, from stress to depression. While most studies have focused on adults, new research shows mindfulness can improve the mental, emotional, social and physical health and wellbeing of young people. Incredibly, neuroscientists have found that long-term practice alters the structure and function of the brain to improve the quality of both thought and feeling.

[8]The whole process of mindfulness has the knock-on effect of making people more receptive and open, What I am trying to do is help them become more aware of themselves in a non-judgmental way. Idea is to strengthen their emotional intelligence and a set of skills that really equip them to cope with everyday life."

According to Katherine Weare, emeritus professor at the universities of Exeter and Southampton's mood disorder center, one of the most useful ways of practicing mindfulness is to take a very short pause in the middle of whatever you're doing. This can be done anywhere by stopping what they are doing, close their eyes and recognize what is happening in their mind and body right now. Grasp your consciousness. It can take just two minutes, but once done, employees are often ready to carry on in a much calmer way.

From Google to the NHS and Transport for London. Even Harvard Business School includes mindfulness principles in its leadership programs. Mindfulness can help to reduce stress and anxiety and conflict, and increase resilience and emotional intelligence, while improving communication in the workplace.

When trying to decide whether you are mindful, consider the following points. In the last week have you found yourself:

Unable to remember what others have said during conversations?

- With no recollection of your daily commute?
- Eating at your desk without tasting your food?
- Paying more attention to your iPhone than to your nearest and dearest?

- Dwelling on past events or dreading what the future holds?

If you answered yes, the chances are that you're zoning out on a regular basis, spending at least some time on autopilot.

Phase 2

In the current economic climate, employees are being asked to do more with less, working long hours with increasingly heavy workloads. Leading mindfulness academic, a professor of clinical psychology at the University of Oxford, says working in a culture where stress is a badge of honor is counterproductive. "We can spend so much time rushing from one task to another. We may think we're working more efficiently, but as far as the brain is concerned, we are working against the grain. No wonder we get exhausted."

The neurological benefits of mindfulness have been linked to an increase in emotional intelligence, specifically empathy and self-regulation. It's the development of these areas that contributes to our ability to manage conflict and communicate more effectively. Mindfulness also enables us to take a step back and consider alternative perspectives rather than simply reacting to events and using the least intelligent area of our brains to make decisions. Mindfulness helps us to flick the switch back to the smart parts of our brain to put us back in control of our emotions, enabling us to choose a more appropriate response.

Mindfulness expert Mirabai Bush, says: "Introducing mindfulness into the workplace does not prevent conflict from arising or difficult issues from coming up. But when difficult issues do arise, they are more likely to be skillfully acknowledged, held, and responded to by the group. Over time with mindfulness, we learn to develop the inner resources that will help us navigate through difficult, trying, and stressful situations with more ease, comfort, and grace.

"Becoming more aware of your own emotions as they arise gives you more choice in how to deal with them. Mindfulness helps you become more aware of an arising emotion by noticing the sensation in the body. Then you can follow these guidelines: stop what you are doing. Breathe deeply. Show compassion towards your mind and body. Allow them to relax. Respond in the most compassionate way. Thank your body for supporting you all the while." Compassionate and merciful thoughts are like cool breeze in the heat of stress."

A number of well-known companies have implemented mindfulness programs for its employees. For example:

- Apple
- Google
- McKinsey & Company
- Deutsche Bank

- Procter & Gamble
- Astra Zeneca
- General Mills
- Aetna

Regular practice of mindfulness increases the brain's ability to repair itself and grow new neural connections. But the use it or lose it approach to physical exercise also applies to our brains so it's important to practice.

A simple mindfulness practice is the one-minute meditation. Find a quiet place and focus your attention on your breath. If your mind wanders (as it probably will), bring your concentration back to your breath. Then relax as the calm unfolds.

if you look at the large picture, what we are talking about, are all benefits of meditation. If you are thinking clearly, you have solved 80% of your problems. Same applies to employees as well. Question is, as an individual, I can force myself to follow a routine but how do I make sure that my employees are doing the cleansing activity or how do I help them? First it is essential that they should the know the theory behind Meditation (which we have already covered in earlier section of book). Further Sessions can be arranged for free for your organization, please feel free to contact me at 987193801 or ankur1122@gmail.com.

Once the edification is done, what remains is the application. Some organizations have created meditation centers and counselling in the premises only.

However, the effective resolution would be, to do a meditation on your seat for 3-5 minutes after every 3 hours (you can change the frequency as per your requirement). So the mandate should be, there will be a music of meditation (preferably instrumental) for 3-5 minutes on every 3rd hour. No matter what you are doing, just pause and detach yourself from the work for 5 minutes. The desktop and laptops should be locked (this is an ideal situation, however there can be some exceptions like Client calls or presentations). This is an outstandingly easy technique to deploy meditation, but the ground rule is, the senior leadership should also follow it religiously. Because you do not follow it, eventually you will lose the interest so do the employees. People always follow their leaders and they know whether you are serious or not.

These exercise will make sure that employee's extreme emotions are washed away and they will have some time to think clearly. We all agree to the fact that whenever we are high on emotions, we tend to make mistakes. Adopting this simple methodology that too at no cost, is enough to show you the results.

Some of the celebrities who could control their emotions:

For Don Bradman, despite the accolades and the expectation that grew from innings to innings,

Bradman remained grounded and resilient. He never deviated from the original day-to-day thinking of his upbringing. This is exactly in sync with what we described above, since he could control his attractions and detractions, he could be so extra-ordinary.

Ray Charles, Helen Keller, Andrea Bocelli are some of the name to take who were differently abled yet famous personalities. If you ask me, I think the reason why they became famous is that their distractions were limited and razor like focus. Same principle applicable to kids, why we do not allow them to dwell to much sports or entertainment during their exam days. Because we want their thoughts to be focused on studies. Clear thinking is the basic requirement for focused approach.

Chapter 5.7

Institutionalize the Respect for the Company

Phase 1

Like other national symbols — the American flag, the Liberty Bell, the Statue of Liberty — the national anthem conveys meaning about the nation's history, myths and ideals. These meanings evoke emotional attachment to the nation, crystallize identity and help people feel connected to something outside of their own immediate family and community. Therefore, it's not surprising that some people feel offended when they think a national symbol is not being respected. National symbols deserve respect not because they are static representations of unchanging ideals.

National symbols should be respected — but not necessarily in the way most people think. National symbols deserve respect not because they are static representations of unchanging ideals, but because they offer a focal point for diverse societies to express and navigate what it is that unites and represents them. It is precisely because they carry meaning, values and ideals that national symbols are important spaces for debate and transformation.

Now, my question is, why not employees does not respect their working organizations in a similar fashion. because we never tried to control it.

we can get numerous articles on respect at workplace. I think what we have missed the crucial point here is, employee should also respect Organization. It is two-way street. If employer keeps on respecting employee, then employee will not care and eventually take it for granted.

As described above, national symbols infuse emotional attachment. Organization can infuse patriotism for the organization by having an anthem and Flag. Which should glorify the achievements of the company. Ideally, it should be capable enough to push adrenaline distinguishing that company has done for the Society, Nation and more of its glory around social aspect (not to talk about financials).

This exertion will only reap if Flag and Anthem are equally respected by the senior management. Then only lower management will understand its value. Because lower and middle management only follows the senior management. They are the ones who are the prime movers for any cultural change.

A flag would be an additional symbol for the respect, idea is to align the organizational values with the values of society. So when you are flashing flags and singing anthem for the company, people should feel that they are obliged to serve for the society and serving this company is the way to do it. This is the only difference why people love to work with defense forces despite all the difficult circumstances. One organization who has developed this respect for itself, is Mumbai Dabba wala, the tag line, "Ann Daan is Maha Daan" so when people is working for the company they feel great about it and generate pride for the organization.

Please understand that people take pride only when you doing for the society and Nation. Nobody wants to associate with an organization with black spot on it. With these organizations, they might stick with you for money and they take pride in earning money. Through Organizational Anthem and Flag, idea is let people know that the organization is a bless to Society and it is not just a profit making unit, it performs its social responsibilities, not because government has the guidelines, but owes to the society for accepting us with open mind and for it has provided such talent pool to us.

As we have understood the concept of symbols, let see how we can implement them and institutionalize it to DNA.

Phase 2

[9]The unconscious processing abilities of the human brain are estimated at roughly 11 million pieces of information per second. Compare that to the estimate for conscious processing: about 40 pieces per second.

Our conscious processing capacity isn't insignificant, but clearly it's just a retention pond compared to the ocean of the unconscious. And more and more research is uncovering abilities of the unconscious that defy reason.

The first, published in the journal Psychological Science, wanted to find out if the brain can track visual targets even when the eyes are duped into believing the targets aren't there. Researchers at the Brain and Mind Institute at the University of Western Ontario exposed participants to an optical trick known as the "connectedness illusion" that causes viewers to underestimate the number of circles (targets) on a screen.

The reason seems to be that visual processing operates along two paths. The first is the one we're most familiar with—how we visually perceive the world. The second is what our brains are unconsciously up to while we're focused on merely "seeing."

Said lead researcher Jennifer Milne, a PhD student at the University of Western Ontario: "It's as though we have a semi-autonomous robot in our brain that plans and executes actions on our behalf with only the broadest of instructions from us."

That was cool, but the next study--published in The Journal of Neuroscience--flirts with the incredible. Researchers wanted to know if the brain can "see" someone else's actions even when the ability to visually see has been destroyed.

Cortical blindness refers to the loss of vision that occurs when the primary visual cortex no longer functions, generally as the result of injury. There's no longer an ability to visually perceive the world in the sense with which we're most familiar (even though the eyes still technically work), but that doesn't necessarily mean the brain no longer sees.

In this study a patient with full cortical blindness could still react to another person's gaze. While in an fMRI machine, the patient was exposed to gazes directed at him and gazes directed away from him. On the face of it, neither should matter. His visual cortex couldn't perceive any sort of gaze. But the brain scan indicated that another part of his brain definitely could.

The patient's amygdala, the brain area associated with figuring out whether external stimuli is a threat, showed a distinctly different activation pattern when the gaze was directed at the patient than when directed away from him.

In other words, it didn't matter that his visual cortex couldn't catch the gaze—another part of his brain did regardless.

Did you realize in the above paragraph that even unconsciously, our mind register activities? How good is that, if we play organizational anthem whenever a person is switching on the PC or coming to work, on speaker mode with low volume (so that other do not get disturbed).

Air and bow your flag whenever there is any big event. Make this a ritual in your company. Make a strict guideline around these symbols, so that even if people do not like it, they should respect. Asking employees to respect their work place is not a big thing to ask, even small shop keepers in India treat their shops like a holy place.

Manifesting Brand ambassadors

every employee is a reflection of company culture to the world. Every employee is a brand ambassador. It is a corporate social responsibility to develop good citizen. Society should have the perception if the person is working for your company then he can be trusted. It infuses a very positive emotion towards the company. Imagine, a person is thinking of leaving a job and his parents/family should say, don't leave this job, it is so respected company. His kid is proud of the fact, that my father is working in such a great company. Just once incident like we discussed above and whole your efforts have paid back in full.

Imagine, how much loyalty and employee satisfaction would it bring on the table.

In order to implement the above practice, every employee has the responsibility to have a good social image because each of his actions are attached with company name. Any violation of law will be taken seriously (e.g. as low as jumping red lights on roads), wear helmet while coming and going out of company premises. If you attached to any NGO and doing good for the society, it will be showcased within teams.

This proposal may not be the direct way to generate loyalty for the company, but eventually it boils down to pride and loyalty only. It stimulates a positive emotion to stay with the company and that's what matters.

Chapter 5.8

Transforming into Positive Personality

[6]By Roger Federer "It's enough. I can't stand it watching me throwing rackets and embarrass myself in front of thousands of people in a live stadium, so I tried to change, had quite a transformation from a screaming, racket throwing, swearing kind of brat on the tennis court to this calm guy today. It's very important to sort of move on. And I think also losses make you stronger. It's important to learn out of those mistakes and then you become better and the better player, you work harder. A light goes up in your head, you go like, 'You know what? I think I understand now what I need to improve.'

"I always questioned myself in the best of times, even when I was world number one for many, many weeks and months in a row, at certain times during the year I said, 'What can I improve? What do I need to change?' Because if you don't do anything or you just do the same thing over and over again, you stay the same, and staying the same means going backwards. It's important for me to actually hear criticism sometimes because I think that's what makes me a better player and that means someone's questioning me who really cares about me, and I think that's really important in the business world as well.

"Because if you never set yourself goals, you can never question yourself, because you just move from one to the next and you say, 'It's going to be okay.' When things are going great, what more can I do? How much better can I become? How much harder can I train? Almost every time I step on the court today I can maybe rewrite history in some shape or form. And all I can do is give my best. Then it's going to be fine, regardless of the outcome."

There is also another version to it, At 17, my family sent me to see a psychologist': Roger Federer reveals angry teenage phase

To summarize the success of Federer: Federer has won 98 ATP singles titles including a record 20 Grand Slam singles titles, 27 ATP Masters 1000 titles and a record six ATP Finals. Federer was also a Gold Medalist in men's doubles with Stan Wawrinka at the 2008 Beijing Olympics and a Silver Medalist in men's singles at the 2012 London Olympics. Representing Switzerland, Federer also won the 2001 and the 2018 editions of the Hopman Cup, as well as the 2014 Davis Cup. At International level Federer won the 2017 Laver Cup representing Team Europe

That's what a positivity could do, we have the seen the example, let's look into the process of transformation from basic:

source: it's attributed to "The National Science Foundation (NSF)". 70000 thoughts per day by an individual. These thoughts can be broadly categorized into below classes:

Law: Thoughts are eternal and every thought either consume or produce energy depending upon the number of variables, overall impact and frequency of thoughts.

- Necessary thoughts: These are routine in nature and mostly related to daily activities (e.g. bio activities). In these cases, the number of variables are low and the impact of failure is also low. These thoughts consume a very little energy as there is no or minimal analysis needed. For example, when we get up in the morning, we thought of going to washroom, now this does not need any analysis. It consumes a very little energy and overall impact of failure is also low.

However, this will depend on person to person. In case of sport person or patient, particular about its routine and timings then these thoughts will not fall in the class of necessary thoughts. They might have more serious impact. As a result, the number of variables or factors and impact have increased.

- Negative thoughts: these kind of thoughts sap your energy because of simple fact that the variables, impact and frequency are large in numbers. These thoughts radiate negative emotions or depressing emotions and is the primary reason for the soaking the energy. It takes complete RAM memory of our mind to connect the dots as the number of variables and sensitivity (is directly proportional to Impact) are large. More we think about it, more confused we become. now the question is, why are we terming it as Negative thoughts, because it diminishes our ability to see clearly. It is as good as, achieve everything by doing everything.

Phase 1

This is the starting phase of the process, we tend to lose our patience and begging to believe that it is beyond our reach. Self-confidence and Morale down to the bottom. It takes our energy and we feel depleted.

One thing is also to be noted here, that the frequency of these thoughts are really high which adds fuel to the fire. As a result of that we feel tired. We try to run away from the situation and start looking for the escape routes. Hence start a vicious circle of negative organizational culture. We become selfish and start working in silos. Somewhere deep down, we start having concerns about our job. In this phase, this phenomenon has only impacted self and started impacting our professional lives.

We are not ready to take more work, because more work may mean more risk or additional pressure. Devil's advocate says that since you are getting fixed pay, why do I have to put in extra. We want to give only to the extent where we are safe and secure.

Phase 2

Law: you always radiate what you have. i.e. a negative person can't radiate positive energy.

Where earlier phase was mostly turning himself into a negative energy. This phase talks about radiating that energy into universe. Once I have become negative, I will only talk, hear and perform negative activities. It does not matter, what professional boundaries, an organization would like to bring in, I will find my own way to dwell negativity. At this point, I will start talking bad about everything, be it my team, personal life etc. I will all have the issues that may exists in the world, my aura will influence other people in my way.

It is as good as, I am having HIV+ virus. I am spreading it and infecting every other. As a result of that this employee starts a nuclear chain reaction, turning every other employee against to the organization is his/her motto of life.

If he is a team member, he will make sure, he will work less and earn more. For that, he will get into politics, putting other people down. Any person who is performing better than him, is a threat to him so he will try all his level best to pull this performer down. For the person, who is like him, he just has to highlight his inefficiencies or strike a devil's deal.

If this person is reached at mid-level, then it is almost impossible to point him. By this time, he is an expert to all company policies and has got clinical approach to say no to all to process improvements from the teams. He will not care about the organization unless it boils down to his job. His ideal situation is to work in silos (not bothered with Organization policies) and let Management know that Team is performing because of him.

Positive or Motivational thoughts

Phase 1

Beauty of these thoughts are it produces energy. Once we start dwelling positive thoughts, it reflects positive emotions which subsequently releases energy, passion and courage. Where all other types of thoughts consume your energy, these thoughts infuse energy. For example, it is Monday and you are doing your assigned work. You are feeling physically tired and plan to take a quick tea or sutta break. While you are just about to leave the desk, your boss comes and informs you, this is for the national project. These codes are to be presented to Prime minister of India for defense improvements and the timelines are being reduced. So we have to deliver it by tonight.

Now, you just got to know that this project is so huge that it has the potential to impact thousands of lives and it is on a national scale. The success of this project can shift your next honeymoon trip to Switzerland, these thoughts are infused new energy into your body. Now you are not feeling tired anymore. You want to finish this work as soon as possible so that you get extra time to review your work. You just planned to cut your break and resuming where you left.

Now, let's pause and analyze what has happened above. Just before a minute, you were feeling tired and want to get refreshed. Series of positive thoughts gave you adrenaline rush. Please note: we are not considering the physical strength, i.e. if you are hungry, I am not suggesting to eat positive thoughts.

- MS Dhoni been the most successful captain of the Indian cricket team, has this gift of calmness. Do you think, he can have positive mindset while having hundreds of unstructured thoughts rushing through his mind. Hence, Frequency of positive thoughts (thoughts per minute) is always advised as low. (Exception: you might feel very excited and will have rush of thoughts. In that case, there is high possibility that you might miss something and prone to failure. So it is always advisable that you always keep your frequency low.)

Metric	Positive Energy	Negative Energy
Variables	Low	High
Impact	Low	High
Frequency	Low	High

Phase 2

Moving to advanced stage, once you are feeling positive about self. You will start radiating positive energy into universe. The best part of being positive is, it gives you self-confidence and pride. You feel valued and create an inner solar system of producing positive energy. You are not affected by outside turbulences because deep inside you know that you are positive enough to deal such situations. Gives you calm and composed posture. And the bonus is, people start looking at you as a problem solver and stress reliever. Became fan of your style, start following you (of course without telling you). Prognosis are increasingly positive that you will start healthy competition and eventually will benefit organization.

You will create an aura where people will get inspired from you. The culture will be incremented positively. Employees start accepting the change because they know no body is making fool of anyone, they are in good hands, their job is safe and hard work will be rewarded.

Coming back to same example again, do you think MS Dhoni had any specialized talent in his team which did not existed earlier (for previous captains). It is only matter of the fact that he could influence his team positively. He could get the best out of them. One of the newspaper printed his conversations with fellow team members.

Tournament: 1st T20 World Cup, India vs Pakistan

Equation: Dhoni is defending a target, it all came to last over. The batsman (opposite team) has to score 13 runs in last 6 balls to win the game.

Joginder Sharma (the Baller): second ball went for a six and not a very celebrated name in the world of cricket

Impacted metric: Whole country is watching, stakes are high, and it is against Pakistan (india and Pakistan are rivals since 1947)

Variable Metric: there are n types of deliveries that a baller can bowl and there is a risk associate to every type. The baller will either be a hero or down to zero.

Frequency of thoughts: all type of thoughts is rushing through baller mind, what if I bowl a wide delivery or no ball, will I be blamed for that, etc?

Result: India lifted the World Cup

Conversation is recorded in newspapers: It says,

MS Dhoni told me he will take responsibility if India lose 2007 World T20 final, recalls Joginder Sharma

The positive thinking of MS Dhoni has influenced so much that they could produce results. Now imagine if the similar phenomenon is happening in your organization.

How: we all know what positivity could do and its benefits. But how do I imbibe it. let's look into the process. Success comes from positive behavior or approach; positive approach is result of powerful intellect. What is the definition of powerful intellect, is one who knows?

- what is right

- determination to do the right.

What is right comes from the goal of your life, if you aspire to be a vice president of company at the age of 40, then your intellect will guide you to explore the kind of study and work experience you need. You will automatically be directed towards your goal, knowingly or unknowingly. On the other hand, if I do not have any plan, every road is my road. Then I will remain confused no matter what I do. So in our context, we want to be a positive personality. We should be absolutely clear what is the definition of it. The positivity comes from positive personality or positive actions. If you are only thinking good but your deeds are contrary, believe me, you will still be the same, because actions leave lasting impression on soul than thinking. You can't have positivity with cactus tongue. start your day with something positive (not newspaper which only has hatred news). Go for a walk, do meditation, especially before the end of the day, do something for someone else without expecting anything in return. Let the law of karma be on your side. Be polite to others no matter what they do, try it to the extent possible. Forgive others not because they deserve it, because you deserve mental peace. Hatred thoughts are like fire, when you generate them, they first burn you then others. You must have had felt this. Do not let your energy be wasted in pretentious debates. If you think, the argument is going nowhere, leave it and invest your energy somewhere else. Transforming into a positive personality is a best gift that you can give to your loved ones. You can't be harsh for other people and lovely person for the family. It always impacts, how much, is the question. Remember, if you make money with unfair means, in best of the favorable cases it is either will be taken by Doctor or Lawyer.

Key to transform personality is inspiration, history has witnessed some fine celebrities who were initially nothing but once they got inspired, they changed the course of the history. Inspiration can be found anywhere and everywhere -- if you know how to look. Whether it's the words of someone you admire or a typically ordinary occurrence you all of a sudden see in a new light, inspiration is what drives creativity and innovation in every field or industry.

Chapter 5.9

Developing Innovation and Creative Capabilities

Phase 1

Have you ever wondered why some organizations are way ahead from their peers? I phones are 7 or 8 times costlier than Samsung or MI. how did Apple keep on bringing new innovations. Is it derived by just one employee or can you infuse innovation into organization culture.

Did it ever hit you, why musicians like Kishore Kumar, RD Burman were able to produce such a classical music which is fresh even today, why best of the ideas often come to our mind in the washroom or quiet place? Newton was sitting beneath the tree and apple fell on him and suddenly he got the riddle. Archimedes when discovered displacement of water, he was in the bathtub. In fact, when you go for a vacation, you tend to forget everything even at times the laptop passwords but you go into childhood memories. do we have conclusion to draw out of it? Why best of the ideas comes from bathrooms?

Above cases answer this mystery of developing innovation capabilities. Below traits are very useful in creating innovative mindset:

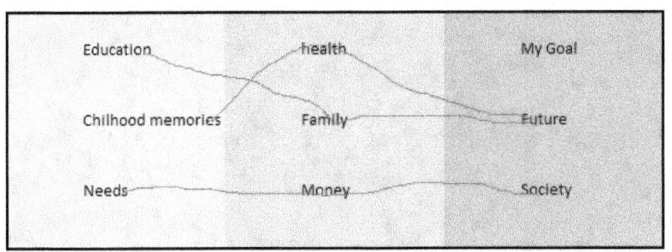

State of Mind

- Clarity of thoughts and Ability to connect dots to see the larger picture: process of innovation is all about to be able to connect several dots in the mind, clarity of thoughts act as a catalyst. For a person to be able to innovate, at least he should be able to connect dots. Enough is being said about clarity already in the previous chapters. It is about the effort that you can put to bring your mind and thoughts in discipline. That is the precise reason why great celebrities are so particular about their schedule. They never allow their mind and thoughts to linger on small issues, thereby saving the energy. Too much affection and too much hatred are dangerous for a healthy mind. You should know the art of moving on with life and leave the past behind. this ability may also be measured in terms of IQ (intelligent quotient). More clarity you have, more swiftly you will be able to resolve and react to the situation. This is the prime difference between great personalities (i.e. scientists) and common man. With this power, you also need the power to imagine.

- **Imagine the future**: when people were really happy with cars and other vehicles. Wright brothers were thinking of flying in the air. It is their great ability to visualize a world with people flying in the mind first and then implementing. Wilbur and Orville Wright were American inventors and pioneers of aviation. In 1903 the Wright brothers achieved the first powered, sustained and controlled airplane flight; they surpassed their own milestone two years later when they built and flew the first fully practical airplane. Every soul is capable of generating thoughts but not everybody is capable of thinking clearly and connect various variables. Just imagine if I ask you to visualize if you are planet Jupiter for one day what are you going to do. It is a great ability. Every invention that you see today, been once visualized by somebody. One of the great batsman, Mr Sachin Tendukar, once revealed that before going for a match, he always visualizes himself as hitting century in that vary match. He is also known as GOD of Cricket. In India, people may not know the who is president of India but they will tell you that Sachin has scored 100 centuries.

- **Ability to stop thoughts and change the direction**: the best way to understand the importance of this feature is, can you even think of innovating something when you are with your crush. That's why this skill is of utmost importance, you can't be thinking about the subject all the time, you would need break and after that, you would need to come back to it. Being creative or innovative needs concentration and relaxation at the same time. Because the faculties of mind are only available when you are at ease.

- **Self-Confidence**: needless to say, before you even think of being creative, you should have the Self-confidence. What is self-confidence, knowing oneself that we are soul and innate capability of doing anything gives us the stable confidence. If your confidence is dependent upon the praise you get from others. You are bound to fail, if not today then tomorrow. Or you have really lucky, to have people who constantly praise you. it is today's era challenges, your self-confidence should be self-generated and independent of the facts what is happening outside.

- **Domain expertise**: I am a commerce graduate; I can't innovate on how the NASA should build a satellite at cheaper cost. If you working in a process, you should know the complete process (End to End) or at least your own activity with purpose (of why we are doing it). Domain expertise is must for any innovation, best way to develop domain expertise is through internal Job transfers or cross training. More people know about the complete process, more they can contribute. The attrition % in this case should be very low. New employee will have its learning curve and will not be in a position of innovating.

If you closely observe the above listed abilities for innovation and creativity, they all are product of your 2 factors, i.e. quality of thoughts, strong determination of mind.

People will tell you different ways to do it, but at the core, it is always how well you manage your input (the quality of thoughts) and mind against your pull and push.

Phase 2

In order to develop innovation and creative capabilities in the organization, below initiatives may come handy:

Displaying tree of thought process of leadership: it is a part of theory of zero salary to have a common vision among all employees. Leadership should be able to communicate their vision clearly. Each and every employee (at all levels) should know the business priority. Sign boards should be placed everywhere to show a complete tree of drilling down the leadership priorities to subtlest level of action or BAU (Business as usual) profile for production guys. This will ensure that the people should know the direction of progress whether they are contributing to the prosperity or not.

Installing Domain expertise: whenever a production employee is working for a process, the best practice is to give him a SOP (statement of procedures) so that he can focus on his work and knows his steps clearly. Simultaneously, why not we tell that employee that how your process is overall contributing to the business objectives. What are the ripples and consequences of an error? Giving them the end to end visibility is another way of sharing the responsibility. This initiative has a lot of advantages, employee will feel connected, he will be able to give better ideas of improvement since he knows the compete process, this is like providing a platform at junior levels to unleash their creativity and innovative skills.

If you have setup above 2 pointers then congratulations, the runway is set for takeoff. One of founding principle to foster creativity is keeping the employee mentally relaxed by focusing on only business objectives. You would want people to stay productive than busy. You should know what you want them to do instead keeping them busy with something or other. Keeping them relaxed and motivated can be achieved using mindful technique, for which we have dedicated one separate chapter.

Chapter 5.10

Trust Between Employees and Employer

Given the importance of trust in any relationship, business or personal, it's surprising how often it's absent in managerial relationships. The macro-level statistics invariably paint a disappointing picture. [10]The recent Gallup workforce survey, for example, places the number of disengaged employees in the U.S. at 70%, a figure that should alarm productivity experts everywhere.

Why is trust between employee and manager in chronically short supply?

The best form of job security is a culture of trust. The employer should be focused on the fact that he wants to earn money along with the growth of the employees. They should be considered a part of family. If you don't consider them from heart, this pretention would not last long. I do not see any problem in committing to the employees that as long as the company is running, we are not going to shun out any employee. Employer should make employee understand that it is your bread and butter not just of employer. That would mean to share the responsibility of organization growth. Making them accountable. Every employee will have to make sure that the company has a future, take the ownership like you would do it in your own firm and I promise that you will always remain valuable to the company. This is prevalent in big MNCs that is the primary reason for their success. It is difficult to quantify the humongous benefits of employees staying longer in the organization. It may start from Efficiency benefits to cost savings. In the next chapter, we have covered one real life case study to understand this situation better.

Moreover, all business owners can agree on one thing; it's that employee turnover is expensive -- really expensive. According to one article, it costs between 30-50 percent of an annual salary to replace an entry-level employee, upwards of 150 percent for a mid-level employee, and up to 400 percent for a senior or highly specialized employee. Nothing could be better than an employee is constantly working for you over the years. At bad times, you can decrease the salary of the employees that is ok, but shunning out employee is like spoiling the culture. Every good employee will start feeling unsafe and eventually leave so you will have left with the people who could not find job outside. Moreover, considering the history of the organization (that you have shunned employees), no good employee would like to join your organization.

Chapter 5.11

Controlling Attrition

Phase 1

Case Study

"[11]When it comes to attrition, nothing could explain it better than Dominos, at times, it had ~150% attrition. The company is willing to try all sorts of strategies to retain employees _ except paying them considerably more. Paying extra is not a long term and sustainable solution.

While pay is a factor, "bad culture cannot be eliminated by paying people a few bucks more." He believes the way to attack turnover is by focusing on store or people managers _ hiring more selectively, coaching them on how to create better culture, workplaces and motivating them with the promise of stock options and promotions.

High attrition hurts the bottom line. It costs money to recruit, hire & train people, and undercuts service when inexperienced employees don't work as efficiently. It costs Domino's about $2,500 each time an hourly store worker leaves and about $20,000 each time a store manager quits, the company estimates.

After doing some math, he realized Domino's was recruiting and training 180,000 people a year at the time, including those at franchise stores.

Mr. Brandon vowed to change things. He re-named the human-resources department "PeopleFirst."

Mr. Brandon conducted research that showed the most important factor in a store's success wasn't demographics, salary, packaging or marketing, but the quality of its store manager. "When that position is turning over at a high rate, the ripple effect of that is enormous," he says.

Domino's has about 15,000 employees; another 135,000 work at its franchisees. Many are part-timers _ students or workers with other jobs who need extra income and a flexible schedule.

Hoping to pick better managers, Domino's implemented a new test. Those seeking promotion to that job have to take a 30-minute online evaluation of their financial skills and management style. Do they understand terms such as "break even" and "cash flow?" How would they manage a poorly performing employee? Candidates then receive training on their weak points.

Seeking a way to discipline employees without alienating them, he bought a pair of dopey-looking, oversized black-framed glasses. They're called the "mistake glasses" and workers have to wear them when they make errors. The joke is that if you couldn't see what an obvious mistake you were making, you need glasses. "You want to make it like a fun environment but at the same time, you get your point across," Mr. Escobar says. He says no one has ever refused to wear the glasses.

Mr. Cecere, 31, coaches his managers constantly. His stores, he says, are now averaging sales of about $20,000 each week, up from $8,500 four years ago. Often he gives common-sense advice: treat people respectfully, be polite and patient. He hammers home that it's not the pay that makes employees stick around, it's their relationship with their manager. "They can go to McDonald's and make that, they can go to Pizza Hut," he says. "You've got to make sure they are happy to come to work for you."

So if you could notice that Dominos has done below measures to turn the table:

- Better performance management system without alienating culprit (who has done errors)

- Better manager-subordinate relations by training their store managers

- Partnering employees by offering them stock options and promotions.

- Understanding the employee side of story

Phase 2

In nutshell, it can be said that you can save lot money if you are ready to change your consciousness towards your employees. The amount of money that a loyal employee can save can only be estimated once you have loyal employees. My question is, did Dominos spent any major fund. That is the power of theory of zero salary.

let me share another eye opener finding regarding promoting employees internally.

[12]Matthew Bidwell, an assistant professor at Wharton who focuses on patterns of work and employment. He suspected that employers didn't realize how much more they were paying to bring in workers from the outside.

Indeed, Bidwell found that not only do external hires get paid more, but for their first two years on the job, they receive significantly lower marks in performance reviews. External hires are also much more likely to get laid off than are those promoted from within. Bidwell scrutinized seven years of employee data, from 2003-2009, from the U.S. investment banking unit of a financial services firm, which included information on 5,300 employees in multiple jobs, from traders and research analysts to support staff. He also examined data from another investment bank and a publishing company.

The external hires made 18% more than the internal promotes in the same jobs. In addition to scoring worse on performance reviews, external hires were 61% more likely to be fired from their new jobs than were those who had been promoted from within the firm. The external hires tended to have more education and experience than the internal hires, but Bidwell says employers don't appreciate how important it is for workers to know the ropes of an organization. "People don't hit the ground running on day one," he says. "We have relationships in organizations that are key to getting work done and a set of structures and routines we need to know." Knowing where and when to file papers, for instance, or whom to ask about approving a project, can make work much more efficient.

Employers underestimate the time it takes for workers to get up to speed, says Bidwell. After two years, the performance reviews of the external hires caught up to the internal promotes. But sometimes an employee has already moved on, or gotten laid off, before hitting that mark.

Bidwell's study was recently published in a journal called Administrative Sciences Quarterly. After he finished the study, Bidwell says he did some further analysis, of how people in a particular unit were affected by an external hire. Because everyone had to work to bring the new hire up to speed, the performance of the whole unit declined. The silver lining for workers is that bringing in an employee from the outside also tends to raise the pay for everyone in the unit.

Chapter 5.12

Delivering Job Satisfaction by Controlling Thoughts

Organizations invests heavily for job satisfactions of the employees, infosys and Google built huge campus to provide all kinds of facilities to employees to increase job satisfaction level. There is also Mumbai Dabba Wala, who does not provide any additional service (even the perks are really low and flat across the organization). Question is, what is job satisfaction, how one is investing huge money and others are doing without money.

It is about the State of mind is about understanding how your mind works so that you can deal with your thoughts in the right way, rather than reacting to, or becoming a victim of, them every day.

We live our adult life believing that our day-to-day experiences at home and in the office are a product of the situations around us, that there is nothing we can do about them. The reality is that our experiences are based on the thoughts we create in our heads about the situations and then, crucially, how we react to them. A simple understanding of how the mind works can ensure we deal with our thinking in a way that is useful to us.

Here are a few techniques wherein Meditation can be of great help:

Switch off the noise

The biggest thing I have learned is that a huge amount of our time is spent dealing with useless thoughts that fill our heads unnecessarily. This means we can't think clearly and become stressed.

Once we know how to ignore these thoughts and see them for what they are, we can think more clearly and become more creative, less confrontational and work better. So think of your train of thought as a conveyor belt and your thoughts as the stuff on it – take what you want and let the rest pass.

Some of the above topics are already covered in the book, soul is the owner of the thoughts and actions, once you get into the realization of this fact, ignoring the unnecessary thoughts becomes an easy task. The simple way to change the direction of the thoughts is by focusing the importance. While you are reading this book, what if you receive a call from your office and receive new assignment, all your thoughts will be diverted. Because the importance of professional work is of prime importance. This topic is covered in detail in Drainage of thoughts.

Crystal Clear Thinking

Confidence is a default trait in humans – you only have to look at young children to see that it's something we are born with.

What happens over time, however, is that we become distracted by insecure thoughts and take them for real. We then work hard to become more confident, which tends to have the opposite effect.

Think of the mind as a glass of water with sand in it. The mind works best when it's still, and the sand can fall to the bottom and separate. What we tend to do when we are not feeling confident and stressed is that we overwork our minds – we shake up the glass. Subsequently things become less clear and situations become harder to navigate.

So next time you are walking into a room to do a presentation in front of your boss or asking for the pay rise you deserve, try not to work the mind too hard. Let it settle and be calm, and get back to its factory settings.

Encourage Creativity

Creativity isn't something you can force or schedule. Often our best ideas come to us when we are not thinking about being creative or looking for a new idea, say, when we are having a shower or going for a run.

In work, understanding your state of mind allows you to unlock creativity by getting your head into a place where you are open to new thinking and ideas.

Think of the best brainstorming sessions you have had. You get that feeling of buzz and excitement, ideas appear out of the blue — these are a result of a healthy, productive mind. As soon as you start experiencing a feeling of unease, slight irritation or being stuck, you're allowing yourself to get into your own head.

Use your feelings as sensors to navigate around productive and unproductive thinking. If you are feeling good, go forward. If the feeling is not there, reverse and come back to neutral. In practical terms, if creativity doesn't flow don't push it. Take a break, forget about it and your mind will recalibrate itself for fresh thinking.

Chapter 5.13

How to be OK when it is not OK (Emotional Intelligence)

Have you ever thought of an emotional state wherein it is completely independent of outside world? How much stability would it bring onto the table if the leadership is not disrupted by the external events and they can maintain their calm composure. This state might look difficult and far cry, but believe me, by the time, you will finish this chapter, you will have the clear development path and inspiration.

[13]Psychologist Dr. Carey Cherniss has been studying emotional intelligence for a long time. In 1999 he published a paper citing a 19-point case for businesses to pay attention to emotional intelligence, using data from the research of others. Here are a few highlights from that paper to help understand why businesses should care about an employee's EQ.

For example, one study followed the hiring of sales agents for L'Oreal on the basis of certain emotional competencies. These agents outsold other salespeople by $91,370 for a net revenue increase of $2,558,360. If that weren't enough, the high EQ employees had 63% less turnover during the first year than those selected in the typical manner.

In a separate study, a national insurance company found that sales agents who were weak in emotional competencies such as self-confidence, initiative, and empathy sold policies with an average premium of $54,000. Not bad, right? Well, compared to agents who scored high in a majority of emotional competencies, they sold policies worth an average of $114,000.

In a third international study of 515 senior executives, emotional intelligence was a better predictor of success than either relevant previous experience or high IQ.

In the figure shown, she is the administrative head or spiritual head of Prajapita Brahma Kumaris Ishwariya Vishwa Vidyalaya i.e. Brahma Kumaris World Spiritual University. Born in 1916, so currently Dadi is 101 years old. She has been thus engaged since 1937 and also spent 40 years based in London from 1974. At the age of 101, she still continues to give lectures, do meditation, travels to different countries for spiritual conferences; she wakes up at 3 am and sleeps at 10 pm, now still enlightening and inspiring over one million students from around the world.

The EEG(Electroencephalogram) of Dadi Janki continuously showed Delta waves, while she was cooking, while eating, while giving lecture, while doing arithmetical calculations, while taking, while sleeping, all the time!.(Delta brainwaves are slow, loud brainwaves- low frequency and deep penetrating, like a drum beat. They are generated in deepest meditation and dreamless sleep.

Healing and regeneration are stimulated in this state.)

Hope you are amazed to know about Dadi Janki, if you want to be like Dadi then learn Rajyoga Meditation, taught at Brahma Kumaris. And become peaceful.

What is emotional maturity? It is the heightened degree of mind stability where you just become the immune to outer world's turbulences. Like I said earlier, for all of our problems, we always focused on extrinsic world. If a car met with an

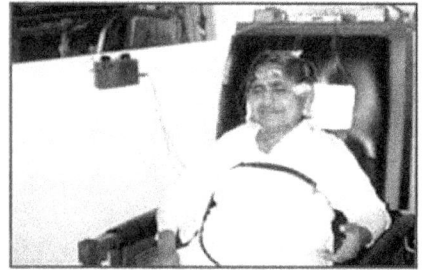

In 1978 Scientists at the Medical and Science Research Institute at the University of Texas, USA examined the brain wave pattern of BK Dadi Janki, Joint Chief of Brahma Kumaris. She was described as the 'most stable mind in the world' as her mental state remained completely undisturbed whilst undergoing tests at the Institute

accident, it is not the car who is at the fault rather the driver. Similarly, we focus on the behaviors of the people and judge them accordingly. Behavior is the just the extrinsic factor, beneath which there are multiple layers. The need of the hour is to focus on nucleus of the problem otherwise we will always be cutting branches will never reach to the seed.

Coming back to point, maturity of the process and people is, to what level of unrest we can accommodate. Process is a product of people thinking so I will focus on people aspect. When we face any adverse situation, it shakes our belief that whether we can handle it or not. The best resolution to the emotional maturity is living inside out. That means, for all needs non-physiological needs, soul himself should be the source. It is a natural tendency to drift towards happiness, love, affection etc. why do we want to look into outside world where everybody is already struggling with so much dynamicity. Why not to build a reservoir in ourselves. I am not saying to become a saint and leave all your possessions and go to jungle. no, this is not the point. Make yourself so rich that even if the world is full of unrest, you should be able to support.

Let's see the difference between living inside out and traditional approach.

Traditionally we have believed that man has physiological needs to fulfil, for that we always look out from the window (soul seeks into world) for what is available. this might have gone well in the past where the resources supply was more and demand was less. Considering the todays world where there is a cut throat competition, world is changing at so rapid pace. Everybody is under pressure to perform. Health disease have evolved to whole new level. Relationships are just social bondage. Everybody is stressed of something or the other. There is no stability in the world. Hence, we are deriving our stability on the basis of the wealth, relationship or professional name and fame, it is almost impossible to remain stable.

The approach should be, first you become the rich enough in values and belief, that even at the time of despair, your positivity should not shake.

Let me share my personal belief with you, I am a soul which is immortal, rest whole universe is made up of five elements of nature e.g. water, air, earth, sky, fire. The worst thing that can happen is death which is nothing but soul changing its room (i.e. Soul changing its body). When I came to this physical body, I did not have any possessions and when I will go, will be empty handed. So what is the fuss. All my relatives and friends are going to be here just in another body.

About my needs, law of karma always prevails, what is sow, so shall I reap. I just have to make sure that I do good deeds because that is what going to be with me even in next birth. Nothing bad can happen if my deeds are good, even if it happening it is because my old deeds were wrong. Because nature or GOD can't do injustice.

What change you think, would it bring to your life, if you practice these thoughts every morning in Meditation? Give it a shot, and you will see the change in 5 to 7 days for 30 minutes.

Chapter 5.14

Psychological Twins

[14]Nothing guarantees mission failure more than a lack of alignment in a senior leadership team. No responsible leadership team wants to be misaligned, but it happens all the time and can be very damaging to the success of an organization. When alignment does not exist, then entire company feels it which in turn will ensure that employees are not connected to a shared sense of purpose. Conversely, when alignment does exist, employees will invest more of their time, talents and energy into meeting or exceeding the goals of the organization. If everyone isn't totally aligned, the employees will eventually receive mixed messaging and start to lose faith in the mission.

Leaders must create experiences that enforce cultural beliefs. And those beliefs must lead team members to proactively take decisive action to achieve specific results. Agree on a shared vision and the results that need to be achieved. When a leadership team is truly aligned on the company's vision it enables the entire organization to have something to get behind. Empowered leaders at all levels can then make decisions based on supporting the ultimate vision. They need to feel connected to something bigger. They need to know that their work matters and is having a positive impact. Once the vision is clearly established and regularly communicated, the team can work towards the results necessary for achieving the vision. A good practice to establish is focused communication from the leadership team about the vision. There is never too much repetition when comes discussing the vision and goals.

Concept of psychological twins means that senior leadership should be so aligned that they should think alike.

Action: To eliminate the complexity, when all senior leadership is pondering on the success of the company. To clear their thoughts, is not it advisable to first clear the pollution (10 minutes' meditation before starting meeting) in the thoughts so that they should think clearly and have same priorities. This stature is absolutely possible considering the fact if we keep aside our personal goals. Meditation can be a great catalyst in achieving that.

Visualizing success together

Great business and military leaders do it. Elite athletes do it. Envisioning what winning looks like is a critical part of achieving success. As Henry Ford once said, "Whether you think you can or whether you think you can't, you're right."

Studies in neuroscience show that when we literally picture ourselves achieving a goal, our brain starts to find ways to get us there. A great exercise to go through once a team has defined their shared vision and goals is to first individually picture what winning looks like and then share those ideas with the team. What does the organization feel like? What will it be celebrating? Going through this exercise is fun and inspiring. It is interesting to see how different team members will envision the win.

Set regular check-ins to stay aligned

A rhythm of meetings and scheduled communication is key for any team to stay aligned. Priorities shift and leaders must be ready to adapt. But all must agree on what the priorities are or need to become. Otherwise varying directives will be coming from the top and chaos will ensue. These check-ins are one of the priorities and must be consistent. Time must be made for those accountable to share updates on progress so that all are informed on where things stand.

Chapter 5.15

Eradicate Negative Politics from Work Culture

As we already discussed, happiness is directly proportional to productivity of the employees. This could be the most significant factor in maintaining thriving culture. Let see what research has to say, about the impact of work environment on health of the employees.

[15]In one research, healthcare and public health professionals are recognizing that the social determinants of health—including where we're born, live, work, play and age—collectively have a far greater impact on our health outcomes than the healthcare delivery system. It's estimated that healthcare services account for just 10% of longevity, while social and environmental factors account for twice that at 20%, genetics 30%, and **individual behaviors an estimated 40%**. Our surroundings and how they influence our choices form the foundation for a healthy lifestyle.

A 2006 American Scientist study on perceptual pleasure and the brain chronicles how being in a high-stress environment such as difficult work environment will cause the brain to signal production of cortisol by the adrenal glands. Elevated cortisol interferes with learning and memory, weakens immune function and bone density, and increases weight gain, blood pressure and heart disease. It also impacts mental health and resiliency by disrupting brain development, triggering emotional problems, depressive disorders, and negatively affecting attention and inhibitory control (Shern et al., Mental Health America, 2014). Toxic stress has been called public health enemy number one, and time in nature can be an effective counterbalance.

Variations of this play out every day. A study done by Robertson Cooper, a business psychology firm, found that in the workplace employees demonstrate a 15% increase in reported well-being when exposed to natural elements such as greenery and sunlight (Humanspaces: The Global Impact of Biophilic Design in the Workplace, 2015). Furthermore, Ihab Elzeyadi's study at the University of Oregon found nearly 10% of employee absences can be attributed to architecture with no connection to nature, such as no windows or views of trees and landscapes (Elzeyadi, 2011). When considering how to improve employee productivity and reduce absenteeism—key challenges that impact company bottom lines—including more windows and natural light, providing open air spaces for walking, and adding greenery on company campuses can make a notable difference.

Hence, it is scientifically proven that mental stress (which is our choice) producing ill effects to our bodies. This is the primary reason why every other professional is struggling for one or the other chronic problems. Having Ego and Jealousy under your belt is first making you sick and then the organization. Forget the humanity, it is about your health that you stay away from it.

Wherever I have worked or conducted training, senior management is either oblivious or does not care about negative politics. Even at times, people told me that it is good for the organization. It is evident if you are enjoying politics that means you are promoting the culture where even if you don't do the hard work or expertise, you should be able to step on others to move ahead. Consider a team of 10 members, all of them are tenured and a new person joins in. This guy is a hardworking and simple in approach. The other 10 will join and play such politics that the survival of this guy will become difficult and eventually he will leave the company or succumb to the culture (he will play safe means no extra initiatives etc.). Who is at loss, it is the organization. Consider such politics in every team, nobody will take any initiative or do beyond his limits. Rather they will invest their energy in conspiring.

Coming back to same old example of have a shell boat. Do you think the boat will move even an inch forward with this crab mentality? Forget about innovation and creativity, even the daily business activities will be hampered. If management can't protect the hard working and honest employee, it may never succeed.

You must have had noticed that people who frequently break the law in own country and when similar people go out of country (developed ones), they become lawful citizen. Because they believe, law is efficient & robust and they will be caught.

If the system is not good, cheating the law becomes a skill. Similarly, if the hard working guy is leaving the company it is the failure of management.

Let's get into the root of the problem, at refined level, it is Ego and Jealousy causes negative politics. Genesis of culture is always Senior leadership and it flows top to bottom or at least senior leadership has the control to impact the culture. The concept should be understood by them, first. Having Ego is like, having a ball of fire. Once you enter the room with ego/jealousy, the other person gets the feel of it and they turn their back to you. Even before speaking you have fallen down to one level to pyramid of transformation. With such approach, people will only do what is required, will not cover extra mile. Reason is simple, leadership is mixing two things, personal Ego and Professional growth. Your subordinates are investing their efforts on your Ego. Claiming respect and giving feedback are different aspect that of Ego. Ego is bottomless glass, no matter how much you fill, it will remain empty.

- Egoistic person theory is, I am superior and others are junior whereas Humility is, I am expert in one area and others are expert in their areas.
- Ego says, either you win or lose, Humility says, win-win.
- Ego says, if your subordinate is countering you then he is insulting you. Humility says, countering is expanding my horizon

- Ego is, I am your boss so respect me that way. Humility is, we all are professionals, we should all be respected for what we do

Other factor that contributes to negative politics is Jealousy, it is envy of other's growth. Fundamental change that we could do, living inside out with imparting belief in the employee's mind that system is justified. Employee should believe that if I work hard, I will get rewarded, and management always supports deserved candidates. Leadership should protect these aspects (i.e. Ego and Jealousy) through policy formation.

Righteous system is already covered in Open appraisal system. Let's look at some of the researches.

The best and easiest way to do it, consider everyone as soul (specialized in their own fields) and try to leverage that potential. You ask Fish to climb a tree and monkey to swim. You will lose them both and eventually will say, I was not having good team. Manager's job is to find out who is monkey & Fish and leadership's job is make such policy so that they do not get spoiled.

Lastly, Important thing to understand is, the Ego is not good for health and business. Egoistic person will be so much occupied with his ego thoughts that he can't focus completely. This is the specific reason you find why most of the very famous persons stay so simple. Because they want to invest it in right direction. If you are egoistic, people will never tell the improvement in your work, even if they do, they will only tell 5% of it. Do you think, is it good for the business?

Some of the measures are shown below:

- Top senior leader should understand the importance of it, culture always flows from the top
- Empower the lowest grade employee
- Manager should be respected in the teams, if he is not then there is a big problem
- Manager main job should be to establish the company policies, clearly. He should have minimum power to influence the rating of the employees. Please refer to open appraisal system chapter
- Manager/Leadership should discourage Ego and Jealousy through policy framework. This is quite a challenge; what kind of policy you would make that would prevent negative politics. How to define it? The easiest way to do it, no employee should be allowed to talk about other employees be it good (because talks can be double meaning) or bad. The wordings could be "we consider every employee is specialized in one of the other subject and the circumstances of each employee differ substantially from one another. Hence, it is not a good practice to talk about other employees in official forum/ meetings. Please refrain yourself form such talks. Incident

reporting (breach of company policy) is an exception."

Chapter 5.16

Servant Leadership (Employees are New Customers)

This leadership style is all about consciousness and everything else is going to remain same. Your people will be your savior, partner in growth. In a time to come, the most critical job of a manager will not be only being an expert in his professional domain but rather able to inspire and motivate people. Indispensability of a manager will be derived from his skill of motivating and satisfying his team members in lowest salaries. There should be extremely strong and uncommon inner desire to serve others. There is an astronomical difference in the performance of the people when they are respected for their skills. A leader with a servant's heart is a truly invaluable asset, and everyone in a leadership position should seek to adopt this type of mentality.

If this approach can be materialized, you and your team can be a great asset to the company. You can absorb extra work and showcase the money save. Imagine one of your member have resigned and other members are willingly ready to accept additional work.

Often times, we confuse leadership with dictatorship. A dictator barks out orders and does not take into account the wants and needs of others. A servant leader is the complete opposite. A servant leader works tirelessly to develop his or her people and is focused on what they can do for others.

I have compiled a few examples of what it means to be a servant leader, and most importantly, ways that you can establish a culture of servant leadership within your organization.

1. **Make sure they know that you care**. We've all heard the famous quote, "They don't care how much you know until they know how much you care." It is crucial that leaders know and understand the message and meaning behind this quote. Being knowledgeable does not make you a good leader, being caring does. Having knowledge makes you valuable for the company but caring, makes you respected. A leader who shows his or her team that they care will not have to worry about loyalty or poor customer service. Place the importance of taking care of your people above the importance of your bottom line. When you take care of your people, they will take care of your customers. Get creative with finding ways to show your team that you care.

2. **Invest in your people.** The biggest investment you can make in your people is your time. Your team wants to spend time with you. Giving your time is a surefire way to let them know how much you care. Spending quality time with your team will impact their job performance directly and

will, therefore, have great impacts on your bottom line. Spend time connecting with them as often as you can. Talk to them about non-work related topics and show genuine interest in them as a person. You'd be surprised how much this will mean to your team. Remember, having a good boss, would mean half of your problems are sorted.

3. Don't place restrictions on your willingness to serve. For a servant leader, no job is beneath their pay grade. If you are in leadership, do not make the mistake of feeling or thinking that you are above grunt work. Your team can sense this type of attitude, and it is off-putting. It also puts distance between you and your team. Never be afraid to roll up your sleeves and go to work.

Believe me, when organizations will understand the importance of this culture, it will become new mandate for team leaders. Even today, pick any company of your choice and you will see the average tenure in that organization is more than 5 years. Operations guys are the ones who are dealing with the customer directly and become the face of the company. You take care of these guys and customer satisfaction is bound to rise. The approach with which we treat operations guys needs to undergo complete paradigm shift.

My point is simple, we do business because we want to earn profits not to demean anybody. In order to leverage the complete potential of intellectual faculties they need to be treated respectfully. *Employees are the new customers* to senior leadership. If they do what they have always done and organization will remain where it is. Senior leadership should focus on employee satisfaction just like Customer satisfaction.

Chapter 5.17

Cariño: Positive Self-Talk

Phase 1

Most of us cannot deny that ultimately we are in control of our own lives once we become adults but many of us don't have a positive mindset. You can choose your state of mind; do you choose to be in a positive state of mind, or a negative state of mind? Many studies have tried to find the secret of success and franchise it for commercial use, and contrary to what people think, it is not the most gifted or even the hardest working who make it. Having a positive mindset is the key.

The only constant personality trait associated with success is a positive attitude. You can learn to change the way that you think, have a positive mindset, learn to focus on the positive, and the ending result turns out much more positive than the times that you allow negativity to enter your mind. All that we can be is according to what we think of ourselves and what our beliefs are. The condition of our mind has everything to do with how our lives are unfolding, and let's not forget that the condition of our mind is a choice.

Remember that where you are now, is not where you will be ten years from now, twenty years from now. You have a very bright future ahead of you; you just don't quite see it yet. So when you find yourself discouraged, get up and take a hot shower, go for a walk, be silly, listen to some upbeat music, dance. You can trick your mind into believing that you are happy, joyful, and motivated, even when you are not, if you try hard enough. Re-focus your mind on knowing that your dreams will come true, in fact, they are just around the corner. You are going to be surprised at how easy it is.

Coming back to our point of discussion, what is self-talk, it is the discussion which one does to himself. Doing self-talk is like starting a nuclear chain reaction, once it triggers, it grows exponentially. It is the self-talk that defines an individual personality. It is imperative that we are always doing the positive self-talk. Not because, it makes us a good or efficient employee but it is vital for happy living. Positive self-talk motivates you whereas negative will put you in depression. Doing positive self-talk is all about conditioning your sub conscious mind. It can fight through your fears of failure and then press on, you can't succeed if you don't try. "You can adopt a growth mindset — and the shift is simply a matter of self-awareness.

Question is, how do I start positive self-talk, it follows a homeopathic approach, means it starts from the basic, it is a discipline about your daily routine. Currently, most people start their day with newspaper or television, which mostly has news about rape, robbery, corruption. Please understand, our subconscious mind is like a small kid, it does not understand the word NO. this is why, the wise people does not brood over the other people's weakness. Because you eventually become the embodiment of that weakness. When you are exposing yourself to negative news, your subconscious mind will start saying that it is a cruel world and people does not deserve good behavior. In this world, you have to be smart, otherwise people will crook you. This is the start of our day, and rest of the day, we treat people and things what we have learnt in the morning.

Law: *We all are creator. Whether you are in happy world or sad world, it is you who built this.*

That's why it is imperative, when start our day, it should start with something positive. Ideal way to start the day, wake up at 6am, do some meditation for 30min, pursue your hobby (go for a gym or something) and then before going to office, read some spiritual journal or attend meditation classes. The simple definition of positivity, it will resonate positive emotions.

Doing positive self-talk means, conditioning your mind, for example, "Today is going to be a wonderful day, thank you God for giving me a chance to showcase my skills. I am the soul is capable of so many skills, let me show some today, I am making a promise that I am will not disturbed no matter what. I will deal all situations with calmness. I will make a conscious effort today that, all my work will be perfect and my interactions will be healthy. I will not have ill thoughts about my peers."

As Darwin says, fittest of the survival, it is the need of the hour that we make ourselves so strong, becomes immune to distractions. You are free to contact author, in case of any help.

Phase 2

Another factor necessary for powerful self-talk is, love for self. Problem is, Love can't be generated with practice then how to develop this.

Soul has a native ability to love for the virtues, it depends on individual to individual. Few people like honesty and caring nature and they felt attracted. Similarly, you should ask yourself what is that virtue which you like the most. Once you identify that virtue, you should start working to imbibe that virtue. For example, personally, I like people who are transparent and good at heart so I try myself to be same. The magic is, if you do it with complete honesty (at times you have to do some sacrifice as well), you will eventually fall in love for self and you will take pride. When odds will be against and world will be firing at you, this important virtue will save you from the heat and boost up the self-confidence. Your inner self will inspire you for good that if you could imbibe that virtue and victorious then you can also win this one.

This is the best form of self-talk that I could ever think of, your deeds and virtues are your real friends, they never leave you alone and are the biggest game changers.

Chapter 5.18

Bell Curve; A Malpractice or Best Practice

[16]The annual performance through Bell curve review was a practice driven by two purposes. The first was to justify salary actions; the second, to motivate employees to higher performance. There were logical and seemingly compelling arguments for each of these purposes. However, one problem got in the way: Those two purposes constantly butted heads with each other.

I am supportive of the need for a dramatic change in performance management, and believe the changes that many organizations are making of late are exactly the right ones.

In 1965 an article, "Split Roles in Performance Appraisal," was published in the Harvard Business Review by three highly respected psychologists who were employed by General Electric: Herb Meyer, Emanuel Kay, and John R.P. French. Not long before, the legendary Douglas McGregor (of theory X & Y fame) had written another HBR article, "An Uneasy Look at Performance Appraisal." Because of the interest this had stirred, the GE team conducted a research on this topic:

1. Criticism by a manager has a negative effect on the recipient. Although employees say they want more information about their performance, negative feedback does damage. No one wants their year's performance converted into a single Arabic digit.

2. Praise does little to change performance. (Later research suggests praise does improve the manager-subordinate relationship.)

3. Criticism generates defensiveness on the part of the subordinate, which in turn leads to poorer performance.

4. Coaching between a manager and a subordinate should occur day-to-day, and not be reserved for a once-a-year event.

5. Goal setting with clear targets and deadlines improves performance.

6. Participation by the subordinate in that goal setting process produces performance improvement.

A few findings that stand out to me are:

- Repeated surveys of both employees and managers have shown that neither group liked the process of performance appraisal. In addition, the higher you moved in an organization, the less likely it was to occur.

- Experts from the quality improvement discipline, amongst others, were constant critics of the negative impact of performance appraisals. Edwards Deming, James Juran, and Peter Drucker were consistent and vociferous critics of it.

- The need to justify compensation decisions was allowed to eclipse the psychological pain inflicted by the appraisal process. Only lately have we had the courage to acknowledge that there is very little distinction between compensation changes for the large group in the middle of bell-curve. In practice, the only people for whom there were real differences in compensation were those at the extreme ends of the curve.

- If everyone in the organization hates the performance appraisal process, perhaps something is wrong.

- Question major assumptions. Performance appraisals being necessary for compensation decisions was, and remains to be, not true. Performance appraisals motivating better performance was a myth that few people believed. However, those were the two major justifications for the performance appraisal practice.
  Microsoft's recent decision to disband its performance management process - after decades of use the company realized it was encouraging many of its top people to leave.

One of the basic assumption in Bell curve is, "we will have a small number of very high performers and an equivalent number of very low performers" with the bulk of our people clustered near the average. In the area of performance management, this curve results in what we call "rank and yank." We force the company to distribute raises and performance ratings by this curve (which essentially assumes that real performance is distributed this way).

This practice creates the following outcomes:

First, we ration the number of "high performance ratings." If you use a five-point scale (similar to grades), many companies say that "no more than 10% of the population gets a rating of 1" and "10% of the population must be rated a 5."

Second, we force the bottom 10% to get a low rating, creating "losers" in the group. So if your team is all high performers, someone is still at the bottom. (The "idea" behind this is that we'll continuously improve by lopping off the bottom.)

Third, most of the people are always in the middle - rated more or less "average." And implicit in this last assumption is the idea that most of the money and rewards go to the middle of the curve.

Does the World Really Work This Way? Is it helping my people growing happier, will they focus on business objectives when they will be working?

The answer is no.

Not sure, what benefit we intend to earn with this approach.

If not this, what should be our approach, because in reality,

"Hyper performers" are people you want to attract, retain, and empower. These are the people who start companies, develop new products, create amazing advertising copy, write award winning books and articles, or set an example for your sales force. They are often gifted in a certain way (often a combination of skill, passion, drive, and energy) and they actually do drive orders of magnitude more value than many of their peers.

The idea should be to everyone to become a hyper-performer by finding the right role for them.

How the Bell Curve Model Hurts Performance?

Right now there is an epidemic of interest in revamping employee performance management processes, and it's overdue. I just had several of my best friends (generally in senior positions) tell me how frustrated they are at their current jobs because their performance appraisals were so frustrating.

Here are the reasons the current models don't work:

1. No one wants to be rated on a five-point scale.

First, much research shows that reducing a year of work to a single number is degrading. It creates a defensive reaction and doesn't encourage people to improve. Ideally performance evaluation should be "continuous" and focus on "always being able to improve."

In fact, David Rock's research shows that when we receive a "rating" or "appraisal" our brain shifts into "fear or flight" mode and shifts to our limbic brain. This shift, which takes place whenever we are threatened, immediately takes us out of the mode to learn or create, making us defensive. So the actual act of executing a performance appraisal itself reduces performance. (Read SCARF for more details: Status, Certainty, Autonomy, Relatedness, and Fairness are what create a secure place to perform.)

2. Ultra-high performers are incented to leave and collaboration may be limited.

The bell curve model limits the quantity of people at the top and also reduces incentives to the highest rating. Given the arbitrary five-scale rating and the fact that most people are 2,3,4 rated, most of the money goes to the middle.

If you're performing well but you only get a "2" or a "3" you'll probably feel under-appreciated. Your compensation increase may not be very high (most of the money is held for the middle of the curve) and you'll probably conclude that the highest ratings are reserved for those who are politically well connected.

Since the number of "1's" is limited, you're also likely to say "well I probably won't get there from here so I'll work someplace where I can really get ahead."

Also, by the way, you may feel that collaboration and helping others isn't really in your own self-interest - because you are competing with your team mates for annual reviews.

3. Mid-level performers are not highly motivated to improve.

In the bell curve there are a large number of people rated 2, 3, and 4. These people are either (A) frustrated high performers who want to improve, or (B) mid-level performers who are happy to stay where they are.

If you fall into category (B) you're probably pretty happy keeping the status quo - you know the number of "1's" is very limited so you won't even strive to get there. In a sense the model rewards mediocrity.

4. Incentives to develop and grow are reduced.

In a bell curve model you tend to reward and create lots of people in the "middle." People can "hang out" in the broad 80% segment and rather than strive to become one of the high-performers, many just "do a good job." This is fine of course, but I do believe that everyone wants to be great at something - so why wouldn't we create a system where every single person has the opportunity to become a star?

If your company focuses heavily on product design, service, consulting, or creative work, (and I think nearly every company does), why wouldn't you want everyone to work harder and harder each day to improve their own work or find jobs where they can excel?

(By the way, internal mobility is a critical part of this model. If I find I'm not very good at the job I'm in now, I would hope my manager will help me move to assignments or jobs where I can become a superstar. Companies that simply rate me a 3 may not give me that opportunity. If we create a more variable and flexible process of evaluation, we have to enable people to move into higher value positions. So having a talent mobility program is critical to success.)

Time to Re-Engineer Performance Management

As I go out and talk with HR guys about this process I'm finding that almost every major company wants to revamp their current approach. They want to make it simpler, focused on feedback, and more developmental.

But in addition to considering these practices, make sure you consider your performance philosophy. Does your management really believe in the bell curve? Or do you fundamentally believe there are hyper-performers to be developed and rewarded? If you simplify the process but keep the same distribution of rewards and ratings, you may not see the results you want.

Look at how sports teams drive results: they hire and build super-stars every single day. And the pay them richly. If you can build that kind of performance management process in your team, you'll see amazing results.

If you think about that one fact, it helps you understand why the "forced ranking" is such a limiting concept and why "continuous development" is the model for organizational success. I personally believe that everyone can be a "hyper-performer" when the conditions are right.

Lastly, my proposal would be, you should do appraisal but need not to follow bell curve, keep the same fund and try to reward teams instead individuals. Let there be a 360-degree survey to find out which team has contributed the most to overall organizational goals. Them within team, who all are at same levels, divide the money in equal portions. There should not be any necessity to downgrade some employees.

Chapter 5.19

Increasing IQ of the Employees

What is the difference between IQ of 162 and 100? IQ 162 will be able to connect the dots and will be able to large picture swiftly than IQ 100. Similarly, if we able to increase the IQ of our employees they will be able to perform better and improve process significantly. IQ can be defined as "Anybody with very high IQ, they have the ability to manipulate, process and interpret information at a deeper level and a higher speed than the average person,".

The current problem is, team member is so engrossed in the doing its daily activities, he does not get any time to improve process. Problem is, how to make him free of his current duties so that he can focus on reducing errors and finding redundancies.

Just like in Lean, we plan to reduce transport and Motion in the process (i.e. 8 wastes of Lean, the Acronym is TIMWOODS). The approach is largely deals with physical motion. What about the effort done by employee's mind in connecting the dots? For example, if an employee is doing invoice processing for AP (Accounts payable) process. As a part of the process, he needs to validate the invoice fields from various systems then use his judgement to take the decision. In this simple process, he needs to check different systems placed in different folders. Since his IQ is already engrossed in doing these activities so he can't think of any betterment of the process. Every Monday, he found himself doing the same mundane job, of which his Manager, does not value him as his subordinate is not adding any value to the work. It is a vicious circle for team members, process and organization. Problem is, how to get out of it. The basic step is, reduce his mental effort and save his IQ, by simply reorganizing the process in such a way, to reduce his retina and brain movement, that will enable him to do more with less thoughts, ideally should be able to do muscle memory. One of the enabler could be to remove subjectivity from the process and bring everything on the same page (to the extent possible).

One of the example is shown below,

Activity	Application used	#Application used	Key Strokes	Application Toggle	Decision based on Data	Decision based on Hunch	Complexity
invoice processing	SAP, Inventory	2	6	6	Yes	Yes	Medium

The idea is to capture above details, and compare them with different processes. By the use of Benchmarking, we can reduce the above numbers.

Any improvement in the above metrics will be great opportunity to improve the IQ of the member. He will invest same time in different activities (may be to understand to End 2 End process). An opportunity for a manager to groom his member and breed employee satisfaction.

Chapter 5.20

Majo; Focus on Grooming, Productivity & Accuracy will Follow

Majo is a Spanish word which means nice. Beauty of this theory is, when it talks about the development of the employees, it also makes sure that these initiatives does not disrupt business processes.

Phase 1

Generic scenario is, people come to office, perform their work and go back home. They work because they want money. To most of the organizations, prime motto is employee should be seen working hard. So everybody joins the rat race, they try to project themselves by pretending as hard working employees. Whether they are actually benefitting the organization is a different question altogether. Periodically, Management does an analysis to understand, how much is the productivity, accuracy etc. Employee gets paid for his/her services and employer is least bothered about anything else about employee. It is either the carrot or stick that gets the work done. During all this, we also push operations guys to do something extra, often, they are reluctant to this approach. Then there are people who are very smart in playing politics.

When all of this was happening, the world has changed. Your client expectations have sky rocketed. If you are doing what everybody is doing, is a threat to your survival. Doing a business, is like a rowing a shell boat. All employees must be aligned to single vision only, otherwise it will not only slow down the acceleration but may also deaccelerate it. Needless to say, money can't buy dedication of the employees. Monetary rewards can only bring performance excellence to a certain level beyond which it becomes stagnant.

Question is, what model should we follow to bring out the best in the employees. Before we began, let me share a story with you, Eklavya was the son of a poor hunter. He wanted to learn archery to save the deer in the forest that were being hunted by the leopards. So he went to Dronacharya (a master of advanced military arts) and requested him to teach him archery. Dronacharya was the teacher of the Royal family.

In those days, as a rule, a teacher to the members of Royal family was not allowed to teach the state art to anybody else. It was forbidden to make anyone as powerful as the princes for the safety of the region.

But Eklavya deeply desired to study under Dronacharya. Dronacharya, bound by the state law, could not accept him as his student.

[17]Eklavya in his heart had already accepted Dronacharya as his Guru. He went home and made a statue of his Guru. Over the following years, with sincerity and practice, he learnt archery and became better than the state princes at the art. He became so good at it that, he would hear the sound of the animal, shoot an arrow at it and claim the animal.

Dronacharya once visited Eklavya, he welcomed his master with great honor and love. He led both of them to the statue he had made of Dronacharya. Eklavya had practiced archery over all the years, considering and believing the statue to be his Guru.

In ancient times, a common practice in learning was- Guru Dakshina, where a student would give a token of gift or fee for the knowledge gained by the student.

Dronacharya said, 'Eklavya, you must give me some Guru Dakshina. You must give me the thumb of the right hand.' Eklavya knew that without the thumb, archery could not be practiced. Eklavya without a second thought gave the thumb of his right hand to his Guru.

Learning: Eklavya felt obliged because Dronacharya groomed him.

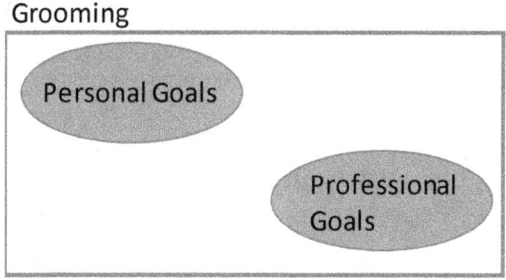

Can we manifest such obligation/dedication in our organization? When we groom our employees, we eventually touching their whole life, professional duties are just one part of it. And our purpose of professional excellence gets automatically fulfilled. Important point to note here, why Eklavya could able to cut his thumb Because he was so obliged the fact his Guru has groomed him. No matter how old you are and how rich you become, people always show respect towards their teachers/professors. That is the another reason why teaching job is so much respected. Teachers are highly respected in China, Greece, UK, Finland. In fact, there was a consensus that for a country to grow, its teaching standard must be world class.

The good news is; the real grooming happens on the job. It is practical knowledge that makes a person earn money. And the bad news is, the employer doesn't get the credit.

Phase 2

If an organization start focusing on grooming their people instead of asking them only productivity and time spent on PC. It makes employees believe that their market value is also increasing hence creating a win-win situation. Manager's job is not just to get the work done but rather inspire and groom people. If we groom our people, it will eventually benefit our organization. Grooming means, enhancement of learning after doing every task. There should be a constant Employee satisfaction survey to check how the subordinates are feeling under their supervisors. Manager appraisal should be done after collecting the survey results from the subordinates (remember the old phrase, people leave Managers Not Organizations). Manager is capable enough to make or break. If he is a good leader, he can make an organization reach new heights otherwise there will always an excuse on why we are down.

Chapter 5.21

Improving Appraisal System

Phase 1

Consider yourself as an employee, who has worked for a whole year, day and night. You have also sacrificed your personal life. Your wife and kids are keeps on blaming you that you don't spend time with them. When you are finally discussing appraisal with your boss at the end of year or six months, you are being told that are given average rating and out of the team of 10 people you are below par.

Now, I consider it injustice, imagine a guy running a 100-meter race. Just close to finishing line, you turn everything black so nobody knows who won. Then you silently call everyone in a room to tell who came first and you also compare their performances of which they have no visibility. This is the prime reason why subordinates don't trust their mangers and felt cheated. Because everybody has given their 100% when asked. When managers give their opinion at the end of the year, it is as if you went to shop, enjoyed the food, now when it comes to paying, you are denying it.

The solution to the above problem is two folds, one is, the manager should define parameters very clearly so that it removes the subjectivity from the system. The success of the parameter is to be judged from the fact that even if manager does not like a subordinate, he still has the chance the scoring the high rating considering the fact he fulfills all parameters. And it should be maintained throughout year. With this approach, you raise the bar. Everybody would know what are the parameters and why they are behind or leading.

Phase 2

The job of the manager should be to make sure the company policies are rightfully implemented without his human bias (based on mood swings, personal likings etc). If this is not the case, as a team member first I have to perform the work and then I will also have to make sure that my manger is happy from me and he is not holding any personal grudge against me. This is dividing my attention means my performance will not be 100%. Part of my energy is also consumed in flattering my manager which is not the goal of the organization.

Law: *Energy or Effort that I put to please my manager is at the cost of effort to my performance.*

Average Handling Time	Attendance	CSAT	Accuracy	Initiatives	Productivity	#Critical Errors	Manager's Perspective	<<<<Parameters
10%	10%	20%	20%	10%	10%	10%	10%	<<<<Weightage
Bench 1	Bench 2	Bench 3	Bench 4	Bench 5	Bench 6	Bench 7	Bench 8	<<<<Benchmark

Example of metrics are given above, in this case, manager's perspective only amount to 10% of the overall score, so even if my manager doesn't like me, I can score in other areas and grab good rating. In next level, we might want to break the manager's perspective parameters as well.

Additionally, Team manager's appraisal should also include a survey done on his respective team members. To judge whether the manager was righteous in his approach, do you consider your manager as a guide or mentor, is he contributing to your learning. This survey needs to be done with great caution, because manager has got all the power to influence it.

Secondly, while doing one to one, ask your team members, what are their passion and what have they learn in recent period. Is it the profile they want to work for future or something else? In my initial part of my career, I was working in finance role, I always want to work for strategic planning team. Would not it be good, if you have an organization where people are working in a department where they want to work. I have seen so many teams that person is asking for a promotion that the manager does not have any position for his promotion or manager does not like him very much because of issues in the past (e.g. ego clashes). Now, this is a very difficult position for a team member, he is not allowed to move out of the team because he is too valuable nor he can get a promotion inside. Prognosis are highly negative; this member has to leave company. Is not it a loss to the organization? Why not we create a win-win situation for manager and member. The answer to this puzzle is **IJM (internal Job movement)**. Stronger these movements are, less are the chances of manager subordinate issues. Because manager will always have this thought in his mind, if I don't value my member, he can move to different team and I will have to suffer the brunt.

Have a controlled yet structured plan for IJP, so that it should not disrupt the process functioning. Transfer people within departments as per their choices. Imagine the amount of cross training we would have; the person will never leave your organization. This would new perspective to the process, fresh improvement ideas on the table.

Chapter 5.22

Déjà vu of Errors

This aspect is bit on the process front, because if your processes are running fine, it gives comfort to employees. This is one of the example, how to remove subjectivity from the system and conveying fairness in the system.

In an organization, we always have 3 types of processes:

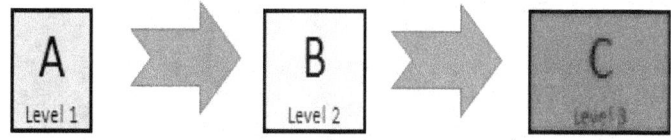

Level 1: Process A, these type of processes has very less requirement of review, if an agent happen to perform any error in any of the transactions, it will be automatically being captured at downstream process. We can say the validations are built in the system in such a way that it will not allow to have any errors. So the error in no conditions will be passed to the consumer or client. It is in the low risk zone, hence marked green. This is the ideal zone where all of our processes should reside.

Level 2: Process B, these type of processes has requirement of review. Every transaction needs to be reviewed, there is an additional FTE (Full time employee) is kept for Quality Check. This is not the ideal zone to have but most of our processes are actually in this zone. The risk in this zone is moderate as review is also happening.

Level 3: Process C, this zone is a kill zone, any error performed in these processes will directly hit the process and quality metrics. All errors will be marked critical by client. And ripples might reach to end consumer as well.

The very reason for performing above exercise is to know where we stand, 1st step should be to bring all my processes under level 1 and second is, in case of those processes which are in level 3, I should deploy my most skillful resources or may be increase audit%. Accordingly, if any of my team member working for level 3 process should be on higher scale of performance.

The objective of this exercise to know the current realm of processes along with their risk factors. Finding out process improvements opportunities and groom my team members so they can pitch in the level 3 process, in case of emergency.

Chapter 5.23

Relaxing at Office, A Malpractice or Ice-Breaker

[18]Japanese economic miracle refers to the significant increase in Japanese economy during the time between the end of World War II and the end of Cold War (1945-1991). Though heavily destroyed by the nuclear bombardment in Hiroshima and Nagasaki, and other Allied air raids on Japan, Japan was able to recover from the trauma of WWII, and managed to become the second largest economic entity of the world (after the United States) by the 1960s (Soviet Union excluded).

Japanese firms encourage their dozy workers to sleep on the job. However, I am not in agreement that employees should be allowed to sleep but let's discuss this. Whenever there are more than 1 human is involved, we are bound to have differences and differences causes mental tension or depression. And that is the prime reason we go for vacations to get some relaxation. What is relaxation, peace of mind with the thoughts and action of your choice. Eventually, you like that place.

The proposal is, why can't we give this relaxation in our offices, so employee will love to be at office rather than going back home (Ideally), of course without hampering the professional curriculum. Can we ask our workers to have some cultural show by each dept. one by one on every Friday for 2 hours and if you are working on that time, you are considered inefficient unless you have approval from VP (vice president)? During this time, you just have to show case your talent, if you do not have it then you have the time to pursue your hobby till your next turn comes. No matter how stressful they are during the week from the work or wife (oops family) they are mandated to pursue their hobby. So they will have thoughts and actions of their choice. The talent could be anything from singing to showing process improvements projects (caution: don't make it a business presentation). Believe me, if you ask them to finish it faster to save 2 hours, they will do it. If nothing is happening, then ask them to do the role play on how this company is changing your life. Make them feel respected toward the organization (as a part of theory of zero salary).

---------Part 4---------

Control or Sustenance

Chapter 6. Control: Not letting the hard work go

Chapter 6.1 Drainage of thoughts and Risk Team

Chapter 6.2 Extending BCP (Business continuity planning) Team's profile

----

Chapter 6

Control: Not Letting the Hard Work Go

Since, we have done so much for our employees, it is imperious that we deploy some control mechanism as well (like every process) so that the employees should not be resort back to their old habits.

6.1 Drainage of Thoughts and Risk Team

In business operations, it is advisable that when you make investments (be it time or money or efforts), always keep a check on it. Likewise, if you are putting effort on employee's development and grooming, it is imperative that the momentum does not break down. Below some of the measures which can help in sustaining the positive environment.

Most of the fun activities are directed towards patriotism, movies, songs etc. Why not to use these activities to foster our desired culture. We can ask teams to prepare a role play on how organization has helped society and nation at large. Why working with this company is a matter of pride? Initially, team will find it difficult, even if they fake it or don't perform it well, I suggest let them do it, eventually it is going to benefit the organization because seeing is believing.

Idea is, employee should not start enjoying negative talks about company and its policies. So keep them busy and constantly hammering the thoughts that your organization is your pride. Ever wondered, why the television commercials are paid so much, this is the power of unconscious mind. Our unconscious mind does not understand the word "NO". whatever it sees or think, it will sink in deeper and deeper. That is the idea, have big posters and banners about glorification of the organization. Keep doing fun activities and showcasing that you are working for such a great organization of all times. People talk what they see. Then there will be a time in the premises where no one will talk about bad about company.

6.1.1 Expending Risk Team's profile

I had my fair chance of working with world's best of the companies which are vigilant about the process risk (and other types of risks) and have a dedicated Risk team. Their profile includes preparing a Risk register and have the attestation from the process owner to confirm that the risks are fully understood by operations manager and have the backup plan ready. They keep on refreshing this activity every quarterly basis. The extension of the profile could be knowing how does the risk originates. It starts from the people talking, seeing adverse thoughts about the organization. The risk team should also be involved in identifying those areas where workers could talk and share such things e.g. Cafeteria, break out area etc. use posters, slogans to glorify the image of the organization because seeing is believing. They can't close their eyes on those slogans. No matter what they do it is going to influence their unconscious mind. In next level, Risk team may also identify the resources who are particularly talking bad about the organization and get their team leaders informed. Do counseling to see what went wrong with them, how can we change their attitude towards work.

Chapter 6.2

Extending BCP (Business Continuity Planning) Team's Profile

Phase 1

Profile of BCP team is to make sure that in case of any catastrophes (e.g. flood, earthquake, riots, world war etc), the organization business as usual does not get impacted and increase resilience. They do all the backup systems available, identify the critical resources and number of resources, back up location etc. While they work to ensure that all of their systems are up and running, one of the underlying assumption they have, these resources will be available during those adverse conditions. I increase the degree of adversity by saying, you might have the people available but the banks are doomed so you can't transfer the salary to them nor you have the cash available. Do you still think, this BCP plan is fool proof? If you ask me, I doubt, because the critical employees that you have identified may not be loyal enough and they leave just at the right time and you will have no legal boundaries to protect yourself.

Phase 2

The extension to this profile could be, one of the outcome of theory of zero salary would be, one should be able to identify the employees who are loyal and will be there to serve the organization even if they are not paid for 3 or 6 months (of course with domain expertise). This might need frequent training and meditation sessions to manifest loyalty and dedication. Demonstrating loyalty is an intrinsic phenomenon and can't be bought or sold. Loyal employees are the only savior during the BCP situations of organizations, they are like life boat on a ship. They are significantly more likely to work to make their organization successful, execute the company's strategy, and help colleagues with heavy workloads.

This book is a work to lower my obligations toward nature and society. In fact, we all have this moral responsibility. While reading this book, if you are not satisfied with the explanation or wants to have further discussion, please feel free to contact me (Ankur Chaturvedi) @ ankur1122@gmail.com and make sure to include "Theory of Zero Salary" in the subject.

Appendix

1. https://www.forbes.com/sites/forbescoachescouncil/2017/12/13/promoting-employee-happiness-benefits-everyone/#7aea957a581a
2. https://www.forbes.com/sites/stephaniedenning/2018/02/02/the-benefits-of-meditation-in-business/#45814b9e54f5
3. https://www.forbes.com/sites/brentgleeson/2017/04/03/how-important-is-culture-fit-for-employee-retention/#633d3f0b7839
4. https://www.thebetterindia.com/18326/the-man-who-moved-a-mountain-milaap-dashrath-manjhi/
5. http://www.espncricinfo.com/magazine/content/story/728587.html
6. https://www.goalcast.com/2017/04/03/roger-federer-never-stop-improving/
7. https://www.theguardian.com/environment/2017/oct/21/insects-giant-ecosystem-collapsing-human-activity-catastrophe
8. https://www.theguardian.com/teacher-network/teacher-blog/2014/jun/03/mindfulness-class-students-education
9. https://www.forbes.com/sites/daviddisalvo/2013/06/22/your-brain-sees-even-when-you-dont/
10. https://www.forbes.com/sites/victorlipman/2013/10/07/the-foundational-importance-of-trust-in-management/#2f7ae583218b
11. https://www.wsj.com/articles/SB110859140448656895
12. https://www.wsj.com/articles/SB10001424052702304750404577320000041035504
13. https://www.forbes.com/sites/stevecooper/2013/03/18/look-for-employees-with-high-eq-over-iq/#2820d17e6daa

14. https://www.forbes.com/sites/brentgleeson/2016/08/29/6-steps-for-improving-leadership-alignment/#69b2bf4f6326
15. https://www.forbes.com/sites/billfrist/2017/06/15/the-science-behind-how-nature-affects-your-health/#19127a9415ae
16. https://www.forbes.com/sites/jackzenger/2017/10/12/what-solid-research-actually-says-about-performance-appraisals/#5818b8272b59
17. https://www.wisdom.srisriravishankar.org/story-eklavya-devotion/
18. https://en.wikipedia.org/wiki/Japanese_economic_miracle
19. https://en.wikipedia.org/wiki/List_of_cycles
20. https://www.seeker.com/astronomy/nasa-telescopes-may-have-spotted-the-first-exomoon
21. https://starchild.gsfc.nasa.gov/docs/StarChild/questions/question18.html
22. https://en.wikipedia.org/wiki/Hurricane_Epsilon
23. https://starchild.gsfc.nasa.gov/docs/StarChild/questions/question18.html
24. https://en.wikipedia.org/wiki/Gravitational_constant
25. https://phys.org/news/2015-04-gravitational-constant-vary.html

Note: Sincere and Honest Effort is being made to capture all the relevant and respective sources, in case, you could not locate the source, please try and search them on domain names (e.g. forbes.com)

www.ingramcontent.com/pod-product-compliance
Lightning Source LLC
Chambersburg PA
CBHW071536220526
45469CB00003B/805